The Center for Responsive Politics was founded in January 1983 to conduct research on congressional and political trends. This, the twelfth publication of the Center, analyzes ways of increasing access of congressional candidates to the electronic media, while reducing its cost.

Board of Directors

Bethine Church, Chair	Paul S. Hoff
Tom Bedell	Steven I. Hofman
Tim Brosnahan	Peter Kovler
The Hon. Dick Clark	Ambassador Dwight J. Porter
George Denison	The Hon. Hugh Scott
Peter H. Fenn	Paul M. Thomas
The Hon. Orval Hansen	Ellen S. Miller, Executive Director

This report was written by Paul S. Hoff of the law firm of Wegman and Hoff, and by Ken Bernstein, with the assistance of Ellen S. Miller, Cathy M. Pino, Larry Makinson and Herb K. Schultz. The statistical information for this report was compiled by Christopher J. Deering PhD. Assistance in completing the survey was provided by Paul Bradley, Kim Limerick, Lloyd Mintz, Nancy Sellar, and Suzanne Sumpter.

Support for this project was made possible by the John and Mary R. Markle Foundation.

The views expressed in this monograph are solely those of the Center for Responsive Politics.

© 1988, The Center for Responsive Politics

ISBN 0-939715-11-2

Table of Contents

Foreword v

Chapter 1. Introduction and Summary 1
   1. Overview of the Issues 1
   2. Results of the Center's Survey 4
   3. Summary of Recommendations 7

Chapter 2. Reasons for Changing the Current System . 10
   1. Reducing the Cost of Campaigns 11
   2. Improving the Quality of Public Debate 18
   3. Providing Greater Exposure to Challengers 21

Chapter 3. Origins and Nature of the Political Broadcasting Laws 24
   1. The Public Trustee Standard 24
   2. The Equal Opportunities Rule 25
   3. Lowest Unit Rate 28
   4. Reasonable Access 29
   5. The Fairness Doctrine 30
   6. The Public Trustee Standard Under Attack 33
   7. Future Prospects for the Public Trustee Standard ... 37

Chapter 4. Free Media Proposals 42
   1. The Politics of Free Media 43
   2. The Economics of Free Media 46
   3. The Issue of Urban Glut 47
   4. Scheduling Questions 57
   5. Third Parties and Free Media 60
   6. Primaries and Free Media 62
   7. Government Financing of Free Media 62
   8. Recommendations 65

Chapter 5. Discounted Rates and Other Regulation of Political Advertisements 69
1. The Adoption of Lowest Unit Rate 70
2. Impact of Current Industry Practices on Lowest Unit Rate ...72
3. Proposals to Change Lowest Unit Rate 79
4. The Politics of Reforming Lowest Unit Rate 80
5. Expenditure Limits 82
6. Restrictions on Ad's Content 85
7. Ban on Political Ads 88
8. Recommendations 89

Chapter 6. Cable, Radio, and Public Broadcasting 93
1. Cable 93
2. Radio 100
3. Public Broadcasting 101
4. Recommendations 104

Chapter 7. Steps to Promote Voluntary Airing of Election Programming 109
1. Repeal of The Equal Opportunities Rule 109
2. Third Parties and the Equal Opportunities Rule 111
3. Debates and the Equal Opportunities Rule 117
4. The Federal Election Laws and Donations of Free Time by Stations 122
5. The Role of Corporations, Labor Unions and Nonprofit Organizations in Providing Candidate Airtime 124
6. Recommendations 126

Chapter 8. Democracy and the Electronic Media 132

Appendix A A-1
Full Text and Overall Results of the Center's Study A-1

Appendix B B-1
Excerpts from Communications Act of 1934 and Implementing Regulations B-1

Table of Charts

2-1	Money Spent on Television Advertising, House vs. Senate	13
2-2	Cost per Rating Point of a 30-second Ad in Various Markets, 1982 vs. 1988	15
2-3	Television Spending of House Candidates, by Media Market Size	16
4-1	Views of Survey Respondents on Free Media Proposals	45
4-2	Comparison of Congressional Districts and Media Markets	50
4-3	Views of Survey Respondents on Proposals to Avoid Urban Glut	55
5-1	Grid Card for WHAG, Hagerstown, MD, an NBC Affiliate	74
5-2	Grid Card for WDIV, Detroit, MI, an NBC Affiliate	75
5-3	Views of Survey Respondents on Discounted Advertising Proposals	81
6-1	Debates Offered to House and Senate Candidates by Media Type	97
6-2	Level of Spending by Candidates on Different Media	102
7-1	Views of Survey Respondents on Proposals to Abolish the Equal Opportunities Doctrine	112
7-2	Third Parties in the 1986 House Elections	114
7-3	Third Parties in the 1986 Senate Elections	116

Foreword

Political candidates today spend more time and effort raising money for their campaigns than ever before. Most of that money goes to buy time on radio and television stations which are licensed to use a public resource to serve the public interest.

With each election, the high cost of political campaigns increases even more. The cost of candidates' commercials now occupies a greater portion of campaign budgets than ever before. And spot advertisements have become the dominant source of information for the American electorate.

To propose balanced reforms of this system is a formidable task. There are legitimate constitutional concerns and imposing technical difficulties. For over fifty years, our government has regulated broadcasting under the "public interest" standard. The Supreme Court, in recognition of the fact that broadcast frequencies are a scarce national resource, has upheld this regulation against constitutional challenge. But critics now contend that recent technological innovations have cured the scarcity problem, and question whether government regulation of television remains legitimate.

The bi-partisan Center for Responsive Politics has done its homework carefully, and its new monograph provides some exceptionally thoughtful answers to these issues.

Adopting this monograph's proposals will not guarantee us answers to all the political ills of our day. Ignorance, apathy and low voter turnout may still remain. But this monograph is a significant contribution to those citizens who want to preserve the democratic process in a technologically advanced society.

If we merely stand aside and allow current trends to continue, we will end up with the best Congress money can buy.

> Newton N. Minow
> Former Chairman
> Federal Communications Commission

1.

Introduction and Summary

> *Why not ... require that, near election time, both great parties be allowed, without expense, an equal amount of time on the air, to the end that both sides of all issues be fairly and adequately presented to the people?"*

1. Overview of the Issues

The above words were not spoken by a current Senator disgruntled with skyrocketing television costs. They were spoken in 1938 by Frank Knox, Alfred E. Landon's running mate on the 1936 Republican ticket, and his target was radio.

Knox's speech attests to the surprisingly long history of efforts to reform political broadcasting — the laws that govern candidates' use of the electronic media. Over the past half-century Congress has adopted a series of laws regulating various aspects of political broadcasting. These laws have given federal candidates the right to equal time, reasonable access to the airwaves, and discounts on advertising rates. Nothing is more central to a successful democracy than allowing citizens to make an informed choice between candidates. And, as Knox realized as early as 1938, the electronic media play a critical role in helping the electorate make that informed choice.

The potential of radio, television and more recently cable to serve as this country's electronic soapbox has thus long been recognized. Yet, during every election period there are complaints about the way candidates use the electronic media — complaints about spiraling campaign expenditures on paid political advertisements, the lack of substantive candidate appearances on the air, negative advertisements, and candidates who are unwilling to debate their opponents on the air.

As disenchantment with the current system has mounted, commentators and members of Congress have proposed ways to change the laws governing political broadcasting. This study analyzes these proposals, based upon the results of the survey by the Center for Responsive Politics (the Center) of 181 candidates who ran for the House or Senate in 1986.

In some cases, political broadcasting reform proposals have become intertwined with more general efforts to pass campaign finance reform legislation. Since media costs are a major component of spiraling overall campaign costs, many campaign finance proposals focus on reducing the costs of media in order to reduce the overall cost of campaigns.

That nexus between campaign finance reform and political broadcasting reform has rarely appeared stronger than in 1988. During congressional consideration in 1988 of S. 2, the reform bill sponsored by Sen. Robert Byrd (D-WV) and Sen. David Boren (D-OK), Senators from both parties discussed giving political candidates a more significant discount on the rates charged for political advertising. After S. 2 succumbed to a filibuster, Republican Senator Mitch McConnell of Kentucky stated publicly that discounted advertising is likely to become one of the centerpieces of a future Republican campaign finance reform proposal. With Congress groping for new, workable campaign finance measures in the aftermath of S. 2, there may be increased attention to proposals which would control media costs and open new avenues for informing the public.

Further discounting of advertising rates is only one of a variety of proposals to alter the role of the electronic media in campaigns and to reduce campaign costs. Some commentators have echoed Knox's suggestion — that many of the problems with the current campaign system could be solved by granting candidates free broadcast time in blocks longer than commercial length. Proponents believe these proposals, which we call "free media," can help cut campaign costs, make campaigns more substantive, and de-emphasize paid advertising.[1]

Proponents of free media frequently maintain that in exchange for the privilege of holding a broadcast license, a station should give free time to political candidates. As media consultant Robert Squier of Squier-Eskew Communications told the Center, "It seems to me that since the people own the airwaves, we should not have to pay a ransom to the people we have licensed the airwaves to, in order to conduct the most important transaction in a democracy, the election."

The legitimacy and constitutionality of these proposals rest on the requirement in the 1934 Communications Act that broadcast licensees must serve

---

[1] This monograph will focus on proposals to change the laws which govern candidates' media appearances outside of a broadcaster's normal news format. Consequently, "free media" as used here does not mean coverage of a candidate on news broadcasts and news interview programs. That type of free media raises issues, such as press/candidate relations and news media coverage of Congress, that lie beyond the scope of this study.

the "public interest, convenience and necessity."[2] In exchange for the privilege of holding a license which entitles them to broadcast on a specific frequency, they have a responsibility to serve the public interest.

Broadcasters see the issue very differently. In addition to challenging the constitutionality of requirements based on the public trustee notion, broadcasters often assert that the very laws designed to make the political broadcasting system open and fair are responsible for many of the problems with the current system. They suggest that, freed of some of the existing restrictions, they could produce more substantive, informative programming about federal candidates. If broadcasters are correct, reforms which would stimulate voluntary action by broadcasters could be an even more effective way to improve the current system.

Even if the laws remain unchanged, corporations, labor unions and non-profit organizations might take several steps to improve the quality of political broadcasting. If these groups increased their involvement in funding political presentations, they could substantially enhance the role of media in informing the public about political candidates.

Each of these matters is discussed in successive chapters:

● Chapter Two describes some of the problems in the current campaign system which reform proposals seek to address, such as the high costs of campaigns and the lack of substantive debate about the issues.

● Chapter Three summarizes the rationale for the public trustee standard which underpins the political broadcasting laws. The chapter also discusses the origin and impact of the current laws governing political broadcasting, poised as they are between the notion of broadcasters as public trustees on the one hand, and the requirements of the First Amendment on the other.

● Chapter Four analyzes free media proposals that would require broadcasters to set aside at their own expense free blocks of time for candidates. This discussion will examine the practical, political, and economic difficulties that these proposals raise, and possible solutions to them.

● Chapter Five reviews proposals that would reform political advertising, as it exists today. These include proposals that would entitle candidates to a significant discount on advertising rates, and other proposals that would discourage negative advertising or regulate the content of a candidate's ads.

---

[2] 47 U.S.C. 309(a). Other references to the standard appear elsewhere in the 1934 Communications Act, as amended. For example, section 315(a) reiterates "the obligation imposed upon them [broadcasters] under this chapter to operate in the public interest." 47 U.S.C. 315(a). *See also* 47 U.S.C. 303, 307(a).

- Chapter Six looks at the special issues posed by cable, radio and public broadcasting, since these media forms can also play an important role in campaigns.

- Finally, Chapter Seven considers various ways to change the laws governing political broadcasting, including the equal opportunities rule and the Federal Election Campaign Act (FECA), to permit broadcasters voluntarily to provide more free appearances on the air by candidates.

To illustrate the current thinking of various members of Congress on these issues, the chapters also summarize the most relevant bills introduced in the 100th Congress that might affect the role of the electronic media in congressional campaigns.

2. Results of the Center's Survey

In order to obtain factual information about how congressional candidates use the electronic media, and to test their views on a variety of reform proposals, the Center surveyed 141 House and 40 Senate incumbents and challengers. This amounted to nearly 25 percent of all major party candidates who ran for Congress in 1986. Candidates were asked how they used the electronic media during the 1986 House and Senate elections, and how they might want to change the laws affecting political broadcasting.[3] Appendix A contains the complete text of the survey, and its overall results.

The Center's survey and this monograph focus on electronic media coverage of congressional races because such races pose unique problems. Unlike presidential candidates, who draw ample media attention, congressional candidates find it difficult to make their viewpoints known because local broadcasters in most markets must cover several races simultaneously. Whereas televised debates may

---

[3] To ensure a representative sample, the Center used a random sample adjusted proportionally for winners and losers, incumbents and challengers, Democrats and Republicans, and candidates from four categories of media market sizes. Each respondent received a copy of the questionnaire before the interview, and either answered the questions by telephone or returned the form by mail. Respondents were told their identities would not be disclosed in order to encourage them to express their thoughts and opinions freely. Telephone interviews were conducted between November 1987 and January 1988. For winning candidates, the Center usually interviewed the candidate's press secretary, who generally consulted with the member before the interview. Most 1986 losing candidates spoke with the Center's interviewers directly. To protect confidentiality, the feminine gender is not used when a respondent is quoted, because only a small percentage of candidates in the 1986 elections were women.

have neared a saturation point during the 1988 presidential primary season, few observers would claim they saw too many debates between congressional candidates. Furthermore, congressional campaigns, unlike presidential races, are not publicly financed — the candidates themselves must raise all of the money they intend to use for media spending.

The following are some highlights of the Center's findings:

- Respondents were evenly split (45.4 percent yes, 45.4 percent no) over whether they favored requiring broadcasters to provide free time for the use of congressional candidates. However, only 29.5 percent of incumbents supported the concept. The proposal drew substantial support from challengers (60.9 percent), Democrats (57.3 percent) and House candidates from the six largest media markets (68.8 percent).

- Commercial television remains the biggest item in media spending for a majority of congressional candidates. Half (50.6 percent) of all candidates spent more on commercial television than on any other medium. The vast majority of Senate candidates (88.9 percent) relied more heavily on television than on any other medium. In competitive races in the House as well as the Senate, television was also the dominant medium: 87.2 percent of candidates in competitive races said they used television most heavily, compared to 37.4 percent in noncompetitive races. Direct mail (23.0 percent) and radio (17.8 percent) were the next most popular forms of media. In the nation's six largest media markets, however, House candidates relied most heavily on direct mail (53.1 percent), while commercial television (12.5 percent) fell behind even newspaper advertising (15.6 percent).

- The short advertising spot is the staple of political communication. Only 12.7 percent of candidates attempted to buy air time in periods longer than 30 or 60 seconds.

- Only 14.7 percent of the candidates polled were offered any type of free media time in 1986, other than debates, newscasts or news interview programs.

- Candidates are inclined to pay higher rates to ensure that their ads are not preempted. Overall, 54.2 percent of candidates preferred to purchase higher priced, nonpreemptible advertising time rather than lower cost, preemptible time. As a result of this and of other changes in broadcast industry practices, the lowest unit rate law no longer gives candidates the discount intended when the law was enacted.

- Of various conditions that could be attached to any grant of free time Congress decides to provide, a majority of respondents supported a requirement that candidates accept an overall spending limit for the campaign (54.9 percent overall and 48 percent of incumbents supported or strongly supported).

- Cable television has thus far failed to emerge as an important tool for most political candidates. Among respondents, 83.1 percent spent less than $10,000 on cable in 1986, according to their own estimates.

- A plurality (46.2 percent to 38.5 percent) favored requiring broadcasters to provide a substantial discount on advertising rates for federal candidates. Incumbents opposed this proposal by a margin of 48.6 percent to 27.0 percent.

- The candidates polled strongly opposed using federal funds to finance free air time. Only 16.4 percent supported having the federal government pay the cost of broadcast time for candidates, and only 29.5 percent supported postage or newspaper advertising subsidies as an alternative to free air time.

- Candidates strongly opposed repeal of the equal opportunities rule, the law that forces a broadcaster who provides time to one candidate to provide comparable time at a comparable price to that candidate's opponent. Among respondents, 16.4 percent supported or strongly supported repeal; 71.2 percent opposed or strongly opposed repeal.

- Of the 1986 candidates that the Center surveyed, 72.7 percent received offers of broadcast time for debates. In all, 65.6 percent of the candidates who received such offers said they had in fact participated in one or more broadcast debates. The three largest categories according to type of offer were commercial television stations (25.2 percent of all offers), a combination of television and radio stations (22.0 percent), and public television stations (18.0 percent).

- Frequently, debates are not held because one or more of the candidates refuses to participate. Of the 1986 congressional candidates, incumbents proved more reluctant than challengers to debate (39 percent declined at least one debate offer as opposed to only 5.9 percent of challengers).

- Respondents supported (61.0 percent supported or strongly supported) a change in the equal opportunities rule to permit broadcasters who provide air time for a debate to air the program without an equal time obligation to the absent candidate if only one of the candidates chooses to participate. Challengers were more enthusiastic about the change (85.5 percent supported or strongly supported) than were incumbents (39.2 percent supported or strongly supported).

- Most candidates expressed favorable opinions of broadcast debates. Of candidates who participated in debates, 72.4 percent believed the debate helped them. A total of 58.5 percent of respondents supported a proposal that, if Congress required stations to provide free time, broadcasters must provide some of the time for debates (38.2 percent of incumbents and 72.1 percent of challengers supported this proposal).

3. Summary of Recommendations

The Center believes a number of significant changes in current law — outlined below — would enhance the electronic media's ability to inform the electorate about candidates for Congress.

No one of these changes can entirely replace the ubiquitous 30-second commercial, or drastically reduce the cost of campaigns. But, taken together, the Center believes that these proposals would make significant contributions to the American electoral system. Because all of the survey respondents were House or Senate candidates, the monograph limits its discussion to congressional races. Many of the recommendations, however, could also be applied to state and local races.

Among the Center's recommendations discussed in the following chapters are the following:

- Congress should enact a limited free media plan applicable to television. In order to make the proposal workable in urban areas, stations should be able to exercise editorial control over the content of the programs and choose which races to cover. No station would be obligated to cover all the elections in its market. But each television station in the nation should be required to provide a total of two hours of special programming on House races and two hours of special programming on Senate races (if applicable) during the four weeks prior to a general election. Each station's program would appear at the same time on the same nights of the week. Stations could either turn the time over to the candidates to use as they wish, or retain editorial control by producing the program themselves.

- The free media plan described above should be adopted in modified form for radio. The Federal Communications Commission (FCC) should develop guidelines that apply the proposal's principles to radio stations that already carry a significant amount of news and public affairs programming.

- The lowest unit rate law, designed to permit candidates to buy air time at a discount, should be revitalized to increase its effectiveness for candidates appearing on television, radio, or cable. Candidates buying time at a rate which permits the station to preempt the candidate's ad should be entitled to buy this "preemptible" time at the lowest rate at which any other advertiser was able to buy the same time over the prior 12 months (exclusive of summer months). Candidates should be entitled to buy time which cannot be preempted (nonpreemptible time) at a rate 30 percent below the average rate paid by all advertisers for the same time over the past 12 months (exclusive of summer months).

- The lowest unit rate rules should be further amended so that candidates buying time at the preemptible rate may be preempted only by an advertiser willing to pay the higher rates for nonpreemptible time.

- A candidate's right to benefit from lowest unit rates should be contingent upon the candidate participating significantly in at least the audio portion of the ad.

- Congress should clarify by statute that the laws governing political broadcasting on radio and television, including the reasonable access rules that protect the candidate's right to buy air time, apply as well to local cable operators and national cable services.

- Although the equal opportunities rule should not be repealed, it should be amended by limiting its applicability to major candidates (major parties and third parties that received more than 2 percent of the votes.).

- The exemption from the equal opportunities rule for coverage of bona fide news events should be expanded to include joint or back-to-back appearances of candidates.

- If one candidate declines a reasonable offer to participate in a broadcast debate, the station in limited circumstances should receive an exemption from the equal opportunities rule, allowing it to include on the program the candidate willing to debate, without having to provide equal time later to the other candidate.

- Congress should clarify that the prohibition in federal election laws against corporate contributions does not prohibit donations by media companies of free air time to candidates, so long as all major candidates in the race receive equal time.

- The election laws governing general corporate or labor union sponsorship of debates should be clarified so that corporations and labor unions may become more directly involved with stations in sponsoring debates and other informative programming on the air, so long as the station maintains full editorial control.

- Private foundations, corporations and labor unions should increase their funding of public charities working to promote debates between congressional candidates.

- The FCC should resume collecting data on the amount of special election programming each radio and television station airs during an election period.

Before examining each of these points in more detail, chapters 2 and 3 discuss the political impact of the current role of media in congressional campaigns, and the specific legal requirements underlying the current system.

2.

Reasons for Changing the Current System

> *Air time is expensive. So expensive that I believe it warps the campaign process . . . so expensive that it infringes on the rights of free speech and free press guaranteed in the Constitution . . . so expensive that it negates the notion of equal access to voters as envisioned in another era by the Founding Fathers.*
>
> — *Frank Greer,*
> *President of Greer, Margolis,*
> *Mitchell and Associates*

Why should policymakers consider free media and other political broadcasting reform proposals, and what problems of the campaign system do these proposals seek to address?

Frank Knox offered one answer to these questions in his 1938 speech when he advocated free radio as a method of reducing the high campaign costs of his day: "What I have in mind is the cost of radio broadcasting. It has already become very nearly the largest single item in the expense of a campaign."[1] Knox's aim — the control of campaign costs — remains a primary justification for many broadcast reform proposals today.

Supporters of change also cite other reasons. They hope that giving candidates free broadcast time will improve the quality of public debate during campaigns. Reformers also hope proposals might provide more media exposure for congressional challengers who now face nearly insurmountable odds in overcoming the advantages of incumbency.

Any proposals to change the current political broadcasting rules must recognize the variety of different ways candidates use the electronic media, and the varying importance the electronic media play in their campaign. For example, among the candidates surveyed by the Center, one House Democrat spent about

---

[1] *The New York Times*, February 23, 1938.

half of his campaign budget on television and radio advertising to win reelection in a tight race. He relied exclusively on 30-second spots. Another House incumbent faced a somewhat different problem: invisibility. He did not receive any offer of free air time or any offers to debate, nor did he ever appear on radio, television, or cable TV. Because he represents a district in a large metropolitan area, he could not afford to purchase television time in his expensive media market, despite his large campaign war chest.

A third candidate, running for a Senate seat in a large state, spent over $2 million on television advertising, between $100,000 and $250,000 on radio advertising, and an additional $50,000 to $100,000 on cable television advertising. Although broadcasters offered several debates in this race, the incumbent turned down the offers in every case. By contrast, an unsuccessful challenger for another Senate seat in a medium-size state spent no money on broadcast time at all. Running a low-budget campaign, this candidate was scarcely visible to the voters, particularly because his well-known opponent refused to debate. His only communication with voters was through direct mail.

No single reform approach can address all of these different situations simultaneously. Different proposals address different perceived failings of the current system. Nevertheless, each of the proposals we will examine in subsequent chapters seeks to address at least one of the problems identified in this chapter.

1. Reducing the Cost of Campaigns

The Growth in Campaign Expenditures on Electronic Media. The level of spending which greatly concerned Frank Knox in 1938 seems somewhat quaint today. When the FCC began keeping broadcast spending statistics in 1956, all federal state and local candidates, including Presidential candidates, spent only $9.8 million for radio and television broadcasts, a mere six percent of their total campaign budgets of $163 million. In 1986 that combined total was eclipsed by *one* Senate race, the Ed Zschau-Alan Cranston contest in California. Cranston spent $6.2 million on television time and $800,000 on commercial production costs; Zschau spent $6.5 million on broadcast time alone.[2]

The trend toward costly media campaigning began in the 1960s as television began to reach into nearly every American household. This trend was hastened by John F. Kennedy's effective use of television during the 1960 campaign and during his presidency. The year 1964 saw the pioneering television commercials of the Lyndon Johnson campaign — slick and professional efforts

---

[2] Herbert E. Alexander and Brian A. Haggerty, "Misinformation on Media Money," *Public Opinion*, May/June, 1988, p.7.

produced by Madison Avenue talent. All of these elements combined to encourage candidates, particularly in Senate races, to bring their messages to the airwaves. By 1968 this new sophistication was reflected in the amount of money spent on campaigns. Overall campaign spending (national, state and local elections, primary and general) almost doubled from $163 million in 1956 to $300 million in 1968, but broadcast spending increased nearly *sixfold*, to $58.9 million.[3]

This unprecedented jump in campaign costs triggered a wave of interest in media reform proposals between 1969 and 1971. Tradition-bound members of Congress with strong grass-roots organizations, fearing that well-funded challengers could overpower them with TV blitzes, became interested in proposals to curb media costs.

Today, even more than in 1969, campaign dollars pour into coffers of the media, and candidates retain less and less money for traditional modes of campaigning such as organizing efforts, rallies, and get-out-the-vote drives.

In 1986, all House and Senate candidates together spent $451 million on their campaigns. The average House candidate spent $268,000, and the average Senate candidate spent a whopping $2,772,000.[4] With campaign spending climbing to these levels, renewed attention has been given to an important component of this spending, media costs.

Level of Campaign Expenditures on Electronic Media. Isolating with precision the current portion of overall campaign expenditures spent on media is not easy because no authoritative figures exist. The FCC in 1972 stopped collecting detailed figures on media spending and the amount of free time granted by each broadcast station. And while the Federal Election Commission (FEC) requires candidates to report and itemize expenditures, it does not require them to report broadcasting costs as a separate item.

The Center asked respondents to identify by category their level of broadcast spending. As expected, the survey revealed that many House candidates cannot afford broadcasting, especially television advertising. Among House candidates, 54.3 percent spent less than $10,000 on television advertising. Among House candidates in the nation's six largest media markets, 77.8 percent spent less than $10,000 on television.

In Senate races, however, media costs were much more important. Almost sixty-five percent of candidates spent more than $250,000 on television

---

[3] *Dollar Politics*, Washington D.C., Congressional Quarterly, Inc. 1982, p.8.

[4] Center for Responsive Politics, *Spending in Congressional Elections: A Never-Ending Spiral,* Washington, D.C., 1988, pp. 2, 7-8.

alone; 8.8 percent spent more than $2 million. These figures confirm that the level of expenditure on media is much more pronounced in Senate races than in House races. The following chart summarizes the Center's survey results on television spending:

Money Spent on Television Advertising
House vs. Senate

Percent of Respondents Spending:	House	Senate
Below $10K	54.3%	14.7%
$10K-$50K	17.8%	2.9%
$50K-$100K	14.0%	11.8%
$100-$250K	11.6%	5.9%
$250-$500K	2.3%	17.6%
$500K - $1 mil	0.0%	26.5%
$1 mil - $2 mil	0.0%	11.8%
Above $2 mil	0.0 %	8.8%
n =	*129*	*34*

Source: Center for Responsive Politics

Anecdotal evidence from political experts, while imprecise, helps put media costs in perspective. Accounts by campaign managers and media consultants indicate that in Senate races at least half of a campaign budget today typically goes to television and radio. Political consultants told the Center that in *competitive* House races (those in which the winner receives less than 60 percent of the vote) candidates generally spend anywhere from 25 percent to 60 percent of their campaign budgets on broadcast media, depending on the size and makeup of the district. Curtis Gans, Director of the Center for the Study of the American Electorate, told the Center a candidate in a "competitive race" spends, according to his own research, 55 percent of his or her budget on television advertising.

In 1987, the National Association of Broadcasters (NAB) released a study, prepared by Aristotle Industries, on how money was spent in the 1986 House and Senate elections. According to this study, candidates spent $97.3

million on radio and television advertising, or only 21.6 percent of the $451 million in overall campaign spending, a percentage that fell below commonly cited estimates of media costs. The NAB report, however, came under a barrage of fire from scholars and members of Congress, calling the study's credibility into doubt. Rep. Al Swift (D-WA), in Elections Subcommittee hearings in July 1987, maintained, for example, that the study grossly underestimated his own media expenditures.

Another measure of political broadcasting costs is provided by the Television Bureau of Advertising (TvB), a New York organization which issues yearly reports on television advertising volume. Collecting political advertising figures from television stations rather than from candidates, TvB found that in 1986 broadcasters received $161.6 million from all forms of political advertising, up from $123.6 million in 1982. Unfortunately, the TvB figures include not only House and Senate elections but also state and local races, making it impossible to determine precisely how much was spent by candidates seeking federal offices.

Comparable figures on radio advertising in the 1986 *Radio Expenditure Reports* reveal that all political advertising for spot radio in 1986 amounted to $15.3 million. Combining this figure with TvB's numbers for television suggests that federal, state and local candidates nationwide spent $177 million on television and radio advertising time for the 1986 elections.

Whatever the precise figure, it appears that all expenditures by federal candidates for Congress related to electronic media equaled, at a minimum, $100 million in 1986 and could in fact have been significantly higher.

Range of Media Rates. In addition to buying more time, candidates are paying more for the time they do buy. All available numbers indicate that politicians are paying significantly more for 30- and 60-second spots than ever before, at least in part because television advertising rates for all purchasers have been rapidly rising.

In June 1987 congressional testimony, Democratic media consultant Frank Greer submitted figures showing that fixed rate television advertising time in prime viewing hours will cost about twice as much in 1988 as it did in 1982.[5] A chart illustrating this trend appears on the following page. During this same six-year period, the Consumer Price Index rose by only about 25 percent. The average cost of one 30-second prime-time spot in New York is currently $14,000, which adds up quickly during a typical 10-day media buy of 50 to 60 spots.

---

[5] "Fixed rate" refers to the rate for a spot which the station cannot preempt. Though this is the most expensive class of time, as we shall see in Chapter 5, candidates prefer it to preemptible time.

Cost per Rating Point of a 30-second Ad in Various Markets 1982 vs. 1988

State	Market	1982 CRP	1988 CRP (estimated)	% Increase
Arizona	Phoenix	97	200	106 %
	Tuscon	46	59	28 %
Florida	Miami	247	482	95 %
	Orlando	81	162	00 %
	Gainsville	21	50	138 %
	Talahassee	30	70	133 %
Massachusetts	Boston	350	725	107 %
	Springfield	54	88	63 %
Michigan	Detroit	230	390	70 %
	Lansing	47	63	34 %
	Marquette	12	39	225 %
	Alpena	5	19	220 %
Montana	Billings/Hardin	12	43	258 %
	Great Falls	12	20	67 %
	Glendive	5	16	220 %
New Mexico	Albuquerque	56	90	61 %
New York	New York	900	1415	57 %
	Buffalo	123	170	38 %
	Albany	67	113	69 %
	Elmira	12	26	117 %
Ohio	Cleveland	184	260	141 %
	Cincinnati	103	155	50 %
Texas	Dallas	300	550	83 %
	Houston	315	545	73 %
	Austin	32	95	197 %
	El Paso	23	70	204 %
	Amarillo	20	51	115 %
	Corpus Christi	21	48	129 %
West Virginia	Parkersburg	10	40	300 %
Wisconsin	Milwaukee	117	190	62 %
	Green Bay	37	63	70 %
	Madison	25	66	164 %

CRP = Cost per rating point (prime time)

Source: Frank Greer testimony, House Administration Committee, June 30, 1987

The rapid *acceleration* in advertising rates has affected candidates very differently because of the wide *disparity* in rates among different markets. The chart demonstrates the variation of costs for prime time 30-second spots. It indicates, for example, that a 30-second prime time spot that today costs $1,415 per rating point in New York would cost only $16 per rating point in Glendive, Montana.[6] Montana candidates therefore find television almost 100 times more cost-efficient than do New York candidates. In addition, since Montana has only one congressional district, a congressional candidate's television ad in Glendive will reach only constituents. In the New York market, 95 percent of those viewing any given ad will reside in someone else's congressional district.

It is therefore not surprising that the Center's survey revealed that House candidates in smaller media markets spent more on television than candidates for House seats in the largest media markets. In middle-sized markets ranked between

Television Spending by House Candidates By Media Market Size

Pct of respondents spending:	ADI 1-6	ADI 7-25	ADI 26-65	ADI 66 & up
Below $10,000	77.8%	55.8%	42.9%	41.9%
$10,000-$50,000	11.1%	14.0%	17.9%	29.0%
$50,000-$100,000	3.7%	11.6%	21.4%	19.4%
$100,000-$250,000	7.4%	11.6%	17.9	9.7%
$250,000-$500,000	0.0%	7.0%	0.0%	0.0%
n = 129	27	43	28	31

Notes
Media markets are typically ranked by the size of their Area of Dominant Influence (ADI), reflecting the size of viewership in that market. There are 213 distinct ADI's in the U.S., beginning with New York (ADI #1) and concluding with Glendive, Montana (ADI #213)

Source: Center for Responsive Politics

---

[6] Each rating point represents 1 percent of the households with television sets in the media market.

7th and 65th in size, more than 30 percent of House candidates spent more than $50,000 on television, while in the largest six markets, only 11.1 percent of candidates exceeded $50,000 in television spending.

Media Costs and Political Action Committees. The figures cited above suggest that the rise in media costs is partly responsible for the rise in overall campaign expenditures. However, many observers believe the increased number of Political Action Committees (PACs) and the increased size of their contributions to federal campaigns have also caused campaign budgets to escalate.[7]

Whether media costs are increasing because of PAC contributions, or whether PAC contributions are increasing because of escalating media costs, reforms that provide candidates more air time at lower costs could reduce campaign expenses and the importance of money in campaigns. Those who see an especially close connection between the cost of media and the influence of special interests believe that if reforms lowered media costs, they would reduce the opportunity for special interests to exercise undue influence over elections.

Some argue PACs often serve as financiers of last resort to candidates who need air time at the end of a campaign, thus magnifying their influence. Democratic media consultant Robert Squier said in an interview with the Center that, "The late money is money that usually has a special interest in getting something for itself in return for the contribution. The late money in a campaign is almost certainly not just for good government."

Political Advertising's Importance to Broadcasters. While imposing controls on media costs could reduce the price of campaigning, it would not significantly hurt the overall profitability of the broadcasting industry. Media expenditures represent a small proportion of broadcasters' total revenue.

Even if one assumed that all of the televised political advertising counted in the TvB figures came from House and Senate races, these advertisements would not represent a significant proportion of the broadcasters' overall revenue. The $161.6 *million* from televised political advertising represents only seven-tenths of one percent of the $22.3 *billion* in total advertising revenue that television broadcasters received in 1986.

---

[7] Political scientist Thomas Patterson, for example, maintains that "It is the growth of PACs, however, not simply the increasing outlays for television, that seems to have driven the recent escalation in campaign spending." Citing the tremendous proliferation of PACs over the last decade, Patterson argues that, "it is 'money push' rather than 'advertising pull' that has accounted for most of the spending increase." Thomas E. Patterson, "It's Not the Commercials, It's the Money" — *Report of the 1982 Aspen Institute Communications Policy Workshop on Money, Media, and Political Campaigns*, Nov. 7-9, 1982, p. 3.

The radio figures tell a similar story. The $15.3 million spent on radio commercials in 1986 by all political candidates, according to *Radio Expenditures Report,* accounted for barely more than one percent of radio broadcasters' $1.3 billion total spot radio advertising revenues. Political advertising represents an even smaller proportion of total radio and television revenues than these figures indicate because in odd-numbered years broadcasters' political advertising revenues are negligible.

Nevertheless, revenues from political advertising may be vital to broadcasters in smaller market areas. Small market broadcasters rely on political ads, both because they generally lack advertising from large corporations and because in these areas politicians can afford to run more ads. Curtis Gans of the Center for the Study of the American Electorate, told the Center: "Some local stations, in the recession of 1982, *survived* on political ads."

However, the particular small market broadcasters with whom the Center spoke said they did not rely on political advertising to any significant extent, particularly because presidential candidates rarely choose to advertise in the smallest markets.

2. Improving the Quality of Public Debate

During every campaign, columnists and critics lament the disjunction between our high democratic ideals and our harshly negative, or smoothly demagogic election campaigns. The blame for these developments typically is assigned to television, which supposedly promotes image over insight, stardom over statesmanship, and slogans over substance.[8]

Altering the laws governing political broadcasting not only might reduce the cost of campaigns, it also might lead to more debates and other substantive presentations by the candidates, creating a better informed electorate. This is particularly true of free media proposals, and changes in the current law designed to make it easier for stations to stage debates. The goal of these proposals is to provide substantial segments of time in which candidates discuss the issues, and to reduce the importance of the ubiquitous 30- or 60-second ad.

Most commentators fault the 30- or 60-second advertisement for the packaging and manipulation of candidates. The Center's survey indicates the extent to which short spots have become the dominant form of communication in

---

[8] Such complaints are hardly new — political opponents denounced the 1840 "Log Cabin and Hard Cider" presidential campaign of the Whigs' William Henry Harrison for emphasizing image and electioneering over issues.

campaigns. Only 12.7 percent of candidates said they ever attempted to buy air time in periods longer than the standard 30- or 60-second spot. The prevalence of the short spot appears to stem from candidate preference rather than from broadcasters' unwillingness to sell time in longer periods. Although television advertising is structured in short blocks, all candidates in the survey who requested time for longer ads had their request granted.

Because many advertisements are either short "feel-good" spots or negative attacks of opposing candidates, experts argue that the paid political advertisement, particularly at the congressional level, does not provide the public with reasoned debate of the issues.

A statement by former CBS News President Fred Friendly exemplifies this sentiment: "Trying to do complex, substantive issues in 30 seconds or one minute is obscene. I'd almost rather see the networks selling cigarettes again than trying to do issues of peace and war, economic life and survival in spot commercials."[9]

Some political professionals also resent the 30-second format, as Democratic media consultant Jill Buckley observed in 1983 congressional testimony:

> The press says that voters in this country cannot make wise and informed decisions based on thirty-second television spots. They accuse us of using sales techniques more appropriate to selling video games than to informing the American voter. They are right... I find having to tell voters about my clients in thirty seconds offensive. I would prefer not to have to do it.[10]

Not everyone agrees that thirty second advertisements are pernicious. Political Scientist Larry Sabato, who critiqued political image makers in his 1981 book, *The Rise of Political Consultants*, nevertheless defends the format as responsive to public demand: "Like it or not, Americans prefer their political advertisements to be short and sweet; the 'tune out factor,' i.e. channel switching, is devastating for political commercials that are lengthier than five minutes."[11]

---

[9] Neil Hickey, "A Call for Reform: Less Convention Coverage, More Presidential Debates, Free Political Commercials," *TV Guide*, Oct. 1, 1983, p. 35.

[10] Testimony of Jill Buckley before the Task Force on Elections, held jointly by the Committee on House Administration and the Subcommittee on Telecommunications, Consumer Protection, and Finance of the Committee of Energy and Commerce, U.S. House of Representatives, July 21, 1983, p. 59

[11] Larry Sabato, *The Party's Just Begun*, Boston, Little, Brown & Co., 1987, pp. 220-221.

Political consultant Frank Greer told the Center that he agrees: "People primarily get their information from 30- or 60-second spots. They're not going to sit for 15 minutes and watch a talking head candidate."

The often-maligned 30-second format may also be a symptom of the disease in the body politic rather than the disease itself. Certainly a 15-minute speech can be just as demagogic and misleading as a glitzy 30-second ad.

Research by political scientists Thomas Patterson and Robert McClure even casts some doubt on the conventional wisdom that 30-second advertisements do not contribute to an informed electorate. They found that television newscasts often submerge issues in their coverage of campaign hoopla and the candidates' "horse-race," and thus contribute almost nothing to the knowledge of low-interest voters. However, "the evidence also shows that another channel of television communication does inform the less-interested voter — televised political advertising." Voters who had seen ads demonstrated substantially superior knowledge of important campaign issues than those who had not.[12]

Richard A. Josslyn, in a content study of political ads from 1970 to 1976, found that 75.5 percent of these ads contained some issue content (though not necessarily a direct candidate statement on an issue). Almost 20 percent of the ads studied contained specific statements on specific issues. While such issue content seems small, it is higher than the 13 percent issue content of newspaper political articles and the 11 percent issue content of TV network news found in Patterson's research.[13]

Thus, 30-second advertisements are not always harmful or worthless, and with debates and other sources of information, the state of American political debate may not be as poor as critics maintain. Nevertheless, free media proposals which grant time in segments longer than 30 or 60 seconds would certainly represent a new opportunity for the public to assess candidates, and to weigh their views on substantive issues.

---

[12] *Annals*, AAPSS, May, 1976, p. 425. Patterson and McClure speculate that advertising provided more information to low-interest voters than newscasts did because, contrary to common belief, advertising actually has a high issue content, and the issues are repeated over many days in a clear-cut manner. Another study found that voters felt they learned substantive information about candidates' qualifications and issue positions from TV ads. Charles Atkin, Lawrence Bowen, Oguz Nayman, and Kenneth Sheinkopf, "Quality Versus Quantity in Televised Political Ads," *The Public Opinion Quarterly*, Vol. 37, 1973, pp. 209-224.

[13] Richard A. Josslyn, "The Content of Spot Ads," *Journalism Quarterly*, Vol. 55 (1978), pp. 282-287.

3. Providing Greater Exposure to Challengers

The two primary goals for reform of the political broadcasting laws are controlling campaign costs and improving the quality of public debate. However, some proponents also argue that by providing both challengers and incumbents reasonable time to make their case to the voter, free media or discounted advertising rates would help counterbalance the inherent advantages of incumbency. If reformers favor political broadcasting changes for this reason, many members of Congress naturally do not share their sentiments. Whether or not leveling the playing field is a desirable *goal* of reforms, it is arguably an important *effect* of many reform proposals.

During most periods of American history, membership of the House of Representatives has changed substantially according to the public mood of the times. For example, in 1892 the Democrats gained an astounding 116 seats. In the 1932 elections the Democrats, riding Franklin D. Roosevelt's victory over Herbert Hoover, gained 97 seats, only to lose 71 of them in 1938.

In recent years large turnover has become extremely rare because it is very difficult to unseat an incumbent. In 1986, 98 percent of the House incumbents who sought reelection won their races. This capped a two-decade trend of "vanishing marginals," as each year fewer House races remain competitive. Of 42 California House incumbents who ran in 1986, all were re-elected and only two — Robert Dornan and George Brown — received less than 60 percent of the vote.

Many observers believe this has serious implications for democracy. As Russell Hemenway, director of the National Committee for an Effective Congress, told the Center: "The most corrupting influence in Congress is that races are no longer competitive. If we have two-year terms it's because (the House) must be responsive, it must be accountable."

Providing means to ensure that challengers as well as incumbents receive a minimum amount of media exposure would help partially counterbalance several advantages incumbents naturally enjoy.

First, as congressional staffs have doubled over the last two decades, members' offices have become extremely proficient at maintaining contact with constituents and providing tangible constituent services. Shrewd use of the franking privilege provides incumbents a cost-free way to keep their names before the voters on a regular basis, and many members of Congress — particularly Senators — receive regular free exposure on the evening news. One challenger in the Center's survey made this point: "So long as incumbents have access to the media as 'newsworthy,' any attempt to provide equal access is doomed to failure."

Incumbents also enjoy a huge fundraising advantage. According to figures compiled in the Center for Responsive Politics' publication, *Spending in Congressional Elections: A Never-Ending Spiral,* House incumbents spent an average of $370,000 per race while challengers could only muster $135,000, a 174 percent difference in spending that gave incumbents a huge advantage. In Senate races, the difference was somewhat smaller but still significant — incumbents spent on average $3,549,000 while challengers averaged $1,835,000, a difference of 93 percent.[14]

Today's voters, without firm party allegiances to guide their choices, are also more likely to choose an incumbent. Studies of congressional elections show that twice as many voters could name an incumbent House candidate as could name the challenger, giving House incumbents a huge advantage in name recognition that contributes greatly to their success.[15] Senate candidates have not achieved a comparable incumbency advantage because both parties' Senate candidates typically receive a great deal of news coverage.

Finally, pro-incumbent gerrymandering in House reapportionment has apparently increased in recent years.[16]

Only advertising or some other media exposure can raise a challenger's name recognition to the point where the candidate can compete against an incumbent with years of service to the district.[17]

While changes in political broadcasting rules would not eliminate the incumbent's advantage entirely, they would make it more likely that the challenger could achieve the necessary name recognition.

Political media consultant Ed Blakely, with the firm of Smith and Harroff, Inc., told the Center that for a challenger to achieve the minimum name recognition necessary the typical candidate must purchase about 750 gross rating points in each media market. The financial investment needed to achieve that level differs from market to market. For example, in a medium-sized market such as Albany, New York, 750 rating points would cost $84,750. However, buying

---

[14] Center for Responsive Politics, *Spending in Congressional Elections: A Never-Ending Spiral,* Washington D.C., 1988, pp. 16-17.

[15] Gary Jacobson, "The Impact of Broadcast Campaigning on Electoral Outcomes," *The Journal of Politics,* Vol 7, 1975, p. 774.

[16] See Albert D. Cover and David R. Mayhew, "Congressional Dynamics and the Decline of Competitive Congressional Elections," *Congress Reconsidered,* 2nd Ed. Lawrence C. Dodd and Bruce I. Oppenheimer, eds, Washington, Congressional Quarterly Press, 1981.

[17] Jacobson, p. 773.

750 rating points in Miami would cost $361,500, making the task of unseating an incumbent in the absence of free media very difficult.

3.

Origins and Nature of the Political Broadcasting Laws

> *Because the license to broadcast is issued by the federal government, it should be the responsibility of broadcasters to allocate the time to candidates so the public has a chance to evaluate the candidates who are running. Time for candidates should be part of broadcasters doing their business.*
>
> — *A Survey Respondent*

In subsequent chapters, this study will examine a number of proposals to improve the political process, reduce costs, and stimulate more serious political dialogue through improved use of the electronic media. These proposals all build on, or modify, existing legal requirements applicable to broadcasters.

Embedded deeply in the fabric of communication law is the concept that stations have a responsibility as a trustee to the public. In several statutory provisions Congress has sought to delineate specifically how this public trustee standard translates into particular obligations for candidates. Appendix B contains the text of the key statutes and regulations imposing these obligations. This chapter will review the current obligations of broadcasters under these laws, as well as arguments that these rules are counterproductive and an infringement of broadcasters' constitutional rights.

1. The Public Trustee Standard

The public trustee standard had its genesis in the first laws passed to regulate the communications industry. By the mid-1920s, it had become clear that some government regulation was needed to prevent competing radio stations from interfering with each other's signals. In an attempt to respond to the needs of the public without having to resort to excessive government control, Congress passed the Radio Act of 1927. The 1927 Act created a Federal Radio Commission with authority to allocate stations' frequencies, power, and hours of operation, and to grant licenses. The Radio Act not only set the parameters of broadcast regulation, it also required that licensees uphold the "public interest, convenience, and necessity."

That phrase, reenacted as Section 301(a) of the Communications Act of 1934 (the Communications Act) laid the foundation for the public trustee standard. Other provisions of the 1934 statute established the FCC and delineated the relationship between the broadcaster and the government. Section 301 asserts government ownership of all channels of interstate transmission. The federal government dispenses these channels for use, but not ownership, by private parties who obtain government licenses. Section 326 prohibits the government from censoring broadcasting signals. Thus, from the start broadcasting license holders were given a hybrid status; they possess private rights, but public responsibilities.

In the early years of broadcast regulation, the courts consistently upheld the public trustee standard created by Congress and implemented by the FCC. In *F.R.C. v. Nelson Bros. Bond & Mortgage Co.*[1] Congress' power to grant and deny licenses and to eliminate existing stations was affirmed. Further, in the first case challenging on First Amendment grounds the FCC's power to condition broadcast licenses on program format, the Supreme Court held that licensing requirements based on the public interest were not an infringement upon free speech. *National Broadcasting Co. v. United States.* In this decision the Court reiterated the initial rationale for broadcast regulation — government action is needed to eliminate the problems created by unregulated use of the airwaves. In its opinion, the Court concluded that, "unlike other modes of expression, radio inherently is not available to all. That is its unique characteristic, and that is why, unlike other modes of expression, it is subject to governmental regulation."[2]

2. The Equal Opportunities Rule

The Communications Act contains, in Section 315, an important doctrine that is one of the best-known examples of the public trustee standard, and a key part of the broadcaster's current obligation to candidates. Known as the equal opportunities doctrine or, in popular parlance, the "equal time" rule, Section 315(a) states:

> If a licensee shall permit any person who is a legally qualified candidate for any public office to use a broadcast

---

[1] 289 U.S. 266 (1933).

[2] National Broadcasting Co. v. U.S., 319 U.S. 190, 226 (1943). Two years later, in Associated Press v. United States, 326 U.S. 1, 20 (1945), the Supreme Court declared that "freedom of the press from governmental interference under the first Amendment does not sanction repression of that freedom by private interests" and that "the [First]] Amendment rests on the assumption that the widest possible dissemination of information from diverse and antagonistic sources is essential to the welfare of the public."

station, he shall afford equal opportunities to all other such candidates for that office in the use of such broadcast station.

Broadcasters not only must sell or offer free and equal amounts of time, but also must equalize, as nearly as possible, time of day, audience size, broadcast facilities, and costs. In other words, a candidate whose opponent pays $1,000 for one minute of television time between 8:00 and 8:30 p.m. cannot be forced to pay $3,000 for one minute at 1:00 a.m. If a broadcast station furnishes background scenery and videotape equipment to one candidate, it must also make them available to opposing candidates. The requirement applies to all candidates in a particular race, not just to the major party candidates and not just to candidates for federal office.

Under the equal opportunities rule, broadcasters do not have to provide time to any candidate. The rule is only triggered if and when a licensee allows a candidate "to use a broadcasting station."[3] Consequently, stations may avoid having to extend equal time to other major or third party candidates by refusing time to any candidates.[4]

Because broadcasters have always considered their responsibilities to third party candidates extremely burdensome, several unsuccessful attempts have been made to repeal the equal opportunities rule. During the first few decades after the Communications Act was passed, free time proposals usually referred to efforts to modify or repeal the equal opportunities provision to make it more attractive for stations to air political presentations, particularly candidate debates.

Congress in 1959 passed the first extensive amendments to the equal opportunities rule, triggered by an FCC ruling concerning a station's news coverage of a candidate. Perpetual Chicago candidate Lar "America First" Daly

---

[3] A "use" of a broadcast station occurs "if the candidate's participation in the program or announcement is such that he will be identified by members of the audience." *The Law of Political Broadcasting and Cablecasting: A Political Primer, 1984 Edition*, Federal Communications Commission, p. 33 (1984). The appearance need not relate to the candidacy in order to constitute a "use." For example, Ronald Reagan's films, if broadcast during one of his campaigns, would entitle his opponents to equal opportunities, a fact which discouraged stations from broadcasting his movies during much of 1980 and 1984. All identifiable appearances by a candidate -- from a paid commercial to a cameo appearance in "Miami Vice" -- constitute "uses" and trigger the right to equal opportunities.

[4] Since the 1971 passage of the reasonable access doctrine, discussed below, licensees have had to allow candidates to buy some time on their station, but the reasonable access rules do not place the station under an obligation to offer free time to candidates.

(who often campaigned in an Uncle Sam suit) had claimed during that year's mayoral elections that he was entitled to equal time as a result of appearances by Mayor Richard Daley in local newscasts.

When the FCC upheld Lar Daly's claim, Congress quickly amended Section 315(a) to exempt four categories of broadcasts from equal opportunities requirements: 1) bona fide newscasts (such as "The Today Show," "60 Minutes," and religious news programs), 2) bona fide news interviews (such as "Meet the Press"), 3) bona fide news documentaries in which the candidate's appearance is incidental to the documentary's subject (such as a documentary on Massachusetts beaches which contains appearances by Massachusetts Governor Michael Dukakis at a time he was also a candidate for president), and 4) on-the-spot coverage of bona fide news events. As initially interpreted, none of these exemptions were held to include debates.

During the late 1950s the networks lobbied for the ability to offer free debate time only to major party Presidential candidates. The time was ripe for such a change because in the 1960 election, with the retirement of President Eisenhower, neither party would run an incumbent. Congress in 1960 passed a one-time exemption from equal opportunities obligations for debates among presidential candidates during that year's general election period, an exemption which paved the way for the famous Kennedy-Nixon debates.

In the late 1960's, election reform efforts often included the repeal of the equal opportunities doctrine. However, when repeal of the doctrine was included in the Political Broadcast Act of 1970, President Nixon vetoed the bill, in part because he wished to avoid added pressure to debate his opponent in the 1972 election.

In the following year, when the Senate again voted to repeal the equal opportunities requirement as part of the 1971 Federal Election Campaign Act (the 1971 Campaign Act), support for equal opportunities ran much deeper in the House. This was because House candidates, whose districts were often covered by only a handful of broadcasters, were reluctant to allow broadcasters to determine candidate access to airtime. In the end, the House prevailed; the conferees left equal opportunities intact in the 1971 Campaign Act.[5]

In subsequent years, the FCC came under increasing pressure to remove debates on a permanent basis from the limits of the equal opportunities requirements. Responding to a petition by the Aspen Institute in 1975, the FCC expanded the equal opportunities exemption for coverage of bona fide news events to include campaign debates. For a debate to obtain the exemption, the FCC required that it be staged by an outside sponsor (such as the League of

---

[5] Pub. L. No. 92-225, 86 Stat. 3, approved February 7, 1972.

Women Voters), take place outside the broadcaster's studios, be broadcast live and in its entirety, and be broadcast because of a reasonable, good faith judgment that it was newsworthy.[6]

That FCC decision paved the way for the Ford-Carter debates of 1976, sponsored by the League of Women Voters, and for subsequent televised debates of presidential and congressional candidates. Major party candidates could now square off in debates without triggering appearances by third party candidates.

The FCC further relaxed its interpretation of bona fide news events in November 1983.[7] In response to a petition filed by Henry Geller, Director of the Washington Center for Public Policy Research, and the NAB, the FCC ruled that broadcasters may stage their own debates, and that the "on-the-spot" news exemption applies to rebroadcasts aired later than 24 hours after an event. The TV networks and local affiliates have proceeded to stage their own debates, though the League of Women Voters has continued staging debates as well.

As a result of these exemptions for debates and news programs, stations can invite major party candidates to appear in a variety of debate or regularly scheduled news interview formats without having to extend the same opportunity to all other candidates.

3. Lowest Unit Rate

As noted, the Political Broadcast Act of 1970, which would have repealed the equal opportunities doctrine, was vetoed by President Nixon. The bill's "lowest unit rate" provision survived to be included in the 1971 Campaign Act. Lowest unit rate remains law to this day, and is another example, albeit a not altogether successful one, of broadcasters' responsibilities to candidates.[8]

Under this provision, broadcasters during the 45 days preceding a primary election, and 60 days before a general election, may not charge

---

[6] Aspen Institute, 55 FCC 2d 697 (1975), *aff'd sub. nom.* Chisholm et.al. v. FCC, 538 F.2d 349 (D.C. Cir. 1976), *cert denied* 97 S. Ct. 247 (1976). In 1976, independent presidential candidates Eugene McCarthy and Lester Maddox challenged the telecast of the Ford-Carter debates on the grounds that the debates were staged rather than bona fide news events and were covered by the fairness doctrine. The FCC rejected the first claim and held that, in keeping with the fairness doctrine, licensees had afforded sufficient time to McCarthy and Maddox in their overall programming. The Fairness Doctrine is discussed in more detail below.

[7] In repetition of Henry Geller, 95 FCC 2d 1236 (1983), *aff'd sub. nom.* League of Women Voters v. FCC, 731 F. 2d 995 (D.C. Cir. 1984).

[8] 47 U.S.C. 315 (b).

candidates for air time a rate higher than the lowest unit rate charged any advertiser for comparable time. The lowest unit rate means the lowest advertising rate offered or sold by a station for a particular type of advertisement at a particular time. Even if the candidate only buys one spot, the candidate is entitled to any volume discount offered by the station for that class of time. If, for example, a station's lowest rate for a particular class of spots is $200 but one regular, preferred advertiser is offered a long-term contract at $160 per spot, $160 is the lowest unit rate. The idea of lowest unit rate was simply to give politicians parity with the most preferred customers of a station.

Stations must offer the lowest unit rate only for a candidate's "use" of a broadcast station or a cable system. In general, any appearance at all by a candidate on a spot, even if only a brief sponsorship identification tag, is sufficient to qualify as a "use." All candidates — federal, state, and local — are entitled to the lowest unit rate.

Although lowest unit rate is now the subject of considerable debate, its enactment and continued existence reflect a willingness by Congress to limit broadcasters' revenues in order to promote candidates' ability to present their case to the voters.

4. Reasonable Access

The 1971 Campaign Act contained another important broadcast reform that further applies the public trustee concept to political broadcasting. Because the equal opportunities doctrine is triggered only by the "use" of a station by a political candidate, a broadcaster, by simply refusing to permit a "use" by any candidate, could avoid having to give time to any candidates. This option was eliminated by the addition in Section 312(a)(7) of the Communications Act of the reasonable access doctrine, which allows the FCC to revoke a broadcast station license for

> willful or repeated failure to allow reasonable access to or to permit purchase of reasonable amounts of time for the use of a broadcasting station by a legally qualified candidate for Federal elective office on behalf of his candidacy.

Thus, Congress provided federal candidates (but not state or local candidates) an affirmative right of access. Licensees may fulfill the requirement either by selling broadcast time, or by making time available without charge.

In 1981, the Supreme Court in *CBS Inc. v. FCC* upheld Section 312(a)(7) against a challenge by the networks and broadcasters, ruling that the

First Amendment rights of candidates, voters, and broadcasters were properly balanced by the FCC's implementation of the provision.[9] Reaffirming the public trustee concept, the Court noted that "[a] licensed broadcaster is 'granted the free and exclusive use of a limited and valuable part of the public domain; when he accepts that franchise it is burdened by enforceable public obligations.'"[10] The Court found that the reasonable access rule "represents an effort by Congress to assure that an important resource — the airwaves — will be used in the public interest."[11]

Though the Court recognized that broadcasters are entitled to wide discretion under the First Amendment, the opinion gave great weight to the First Amendment rights of voters and candidates. According to the Court, the reasonable access rule "makes a significant contribution to freedom of expression by enhancing the ability of candidates to present, and the public to receive, information necessary for the effective operation of the democratic process."[12]

5. The Fairness Doctrine

Perhaps the most controversial regulation of broadcasters based on the public trustee concept is the fairness doctrine, the chief impact of which is in areas other than political broadcasting. In August 1987, the FCC voted to stop enforcing the doctrine, and to date presidential opposition has blocked legislative efforts to reimpose it.

The doctrine was developed in a series of administrative rulings beginning in the 1930s.[13] As it eventually evolved, the fairness doctrine imposed a two fold obligation on broadcast licensees. First, licensees must devote a reasonable percentage of broadcast time to the coverage of controversial issues of public importance. The broadcaster enjoys a large degree of discretion

---

[9] 453 U.S. 367 (1981)

[10] *Ibid* at 395 quoting Office of Communication of the United Church of Christ v. FCC, 359 F.2d 994, 1003 (D.C. Cir. 1966).

[11] *Ibid* at 397.

[12] *Ibid* at 396.

[13] In early rulings, the FCC required licensees to offer "well balanced program structures, including important public events, discussion of public questions... and news and matters of interest to all members of the family." Great Lakes Broadcasting Co., 3 F.R.C. Ann. Rep. 32 (1929) (ruling by the FCC's predecessor, the Federal Radio Commission). Stations were to avoid excessive advertising, and present "all sides of important public questions fairly, objectively, and without bias." (In re: Mayflower Broadcasting Corp. and the Yankee Network, Inc. (WAAB), 8 FCC 333 (1940)). The most significant of these rulings came in 1949 when the Fairness Doctrine was formally announced. Editorializing by Broadcast Licensees, 13 FCC 1246 (1949).

in deciding which issues to cover, and must only act with "reasonableness" in deciding how to meet its public interest obligation.

The second part of the fairness doctrine required licensees which broadcast one side of a controversial issue, to provide reasonable opportunities for the presentation of contrasting viewpoints. It did not require that, in each presentation of an issue, broadcasters provide *equal* time for opposing views. Licensees simply must ensure that their programming, taken as a whole, presents any controversial issues it addresses in a balanced fashion.

Though the fairness doctrine generally does not specify how broadcasters should fulfill their obligations, FCC regulations do provide some explicit guidelines applicable in specific circumstances. The FCC's "Cullman Doctrine" requires broadcasters who have sold time to spokespersons of one side of a controversial issue, to provide free response time if the broadcaster has not presented the other side and a suitable spokesperson is unable to buy time. If a station broadcasts an editorial it need not present a specific rebuttal, but it must present contrasting views elsewhere in its programming, or affirmatively seek to obtain contrasting views. The FCC in 1967 also drafted specific rules with regard to personal attacks.[14]

Since the equal opportunities rule specifically requires stations to provide equal time to both candidates, and therefore their contrasting views, the fairness doctrine generally adds little to the way stations must cover political campaigns. In one respect, however, the fairness doctrine does directly affect political candidates. The equal opportunities rule applies only to legally qualified candidates for federal office; it does not cover broadcast appearances by a candidate's supporters. The FCC in 1970 addressed such situations by announcing the so-called "Zapple Doctrine" in a response to an inquiry from Senate aide Nicholas Zapple.[15]

Sometimes called the "quasi-equal opportunities doctrine," the Zapple Doctrine combines elements of the fairness and equal opportunities doctrines. Under the Zapple Doctrine, if a broadcast station sells or makes available free

---

[14] When, in discussing a controversial issue of public importance, a licensee broadcasts a personal attack against the honesty, integrity, character, or personal qualities of an individual or group, it must notify the target of the attack and offer an opportunity to respond. This rule, however, does not apply to newscasts, news interviews, or news coverage and, more importantly, does not apply to political candidates or their spokespersons. 47 C.F.R. §73.1920. A political editorializing rule which does affect political candidates provides that if a licensee editorializes for or against a candidate, the opposed candidate(s) must be notified and given an opportunity to respond. 47 C.F.R. §73.1930.

[15] Letter to Nicholas Zapple, 23 FCC 2d 707 (1970).

time to one candidate's supporters, it must make comparable (not equal) spots or free time available to supporters of the candidate's opponent. Like the equal opportunities rule, the Zapple Doctrine does not apply to bona fide news programs and is limited to formal campaign periods. Unlike equal opportunities, it does not entitle supporters of third party candidates to time.

In determining fairness doctrine violations, the FCC does not monitor broadcasts, but instead acts on public complaints. Initially, fairness doctrine compliance was assessed only at the time of license renewal. Beginning in 1962, the FCC undertook to review complaints on a case by case basis. Though the FCC receives hundreds of complaints each year, it has found comparatively few violations, particularly since 1981.[16]

The Supreme Court in 1969 upheld the legality of the fairness doctrine in a seminal case that gave full judicial endorsement to the public trustee standard, *Red Lion Broadcasting Co. v. FCC*.[17] The Court reasoned that given the pre-1927 "chaos and confusion" in the broadcasting industry, the government had the right to intervene and grant licenses to a select few persons: "It would be strange if the First Amendment . . . prevented the government from making radio communications possible."[18] Since the recipients of the licenses had no constitutional right to be chosen for a license or to monopolize a radio frequency,

> Nothing in the First Amendment . . . prevents the Government from requiring a licensee to share his frequency with others and to conduct himself as a proxy or fiduciary with obligations to present those views and voices which are representative of his community.[19]

The Court went on to hold that this government-imposed duty, rather than diminishing First Amendment rights, enhances the value of free speech:

> It is the purpose of the First Amendment to preserve an uninhibited marketplace of ideas...

---

[16] During the six years that Mark Fowler chaired the Commission, only one fairness doctrine complaint resulted in litigation. That case led to a Court of Appeals ruling that the FCC had to consider whether the fairness doctrine is unconstitutional. Meredith Corp. v. FCC, 809 F.2d 863 (D.C. Cir. 1987).
[17] 395 U.S. 367 (1969).
[18] *Ibid* at 389.
[19] *Ibid* at 389.

rather than to countenance monopolization of the market.[20]

Thus, "[i]t is the right of the viewers and listeners, not the right of the broadcasters, which is paramount."[21]

Red Lion did acknowledge opposing arguments that the fairness doctrine might chill coverage of controversial issues, but the Court was loath to overturn government regulation on the basis of unsubstantiated claims: "If experience with the administration of these doctrines indicates that they have the net effect of reducing rather than enhancing the volume and quality of coverage, there will be time enough to reconsider the constitutional implications."[22]

6. The Public Trustee Standard Under Attack

In the almost two decades since the *Red Lion* decision, the courts have issued several opinions which could foreshadow a change in judicial attitude toward not only the fairness doctrine, but the basic validity of the public trustee concept. This in turn could undermine the legality of the political broadcasting rules. In *Columbia Broadcasting Systems, Inc. v. Democratic National Committee*,[23] the Supreme Court upheld an FCC ruling that neither the Communications Act nor the First Amendment requires broadcasters to accept paid editorial advertisements. The decision strongly supported broadcasters' editorial rights, and emphasized that regulations affecting the broadcaster's right of free speech must pass a balancing test.

A year later, the Supreme Court struck down a Florida statute requiring newspapers to provide free space to political candidates attacked in their editorials. In *Miami Herald Publishing Co. v. Tornillo,* the Court held that the First Amendment guarantees of a free press prohibit government interference in newspaper editors' decisions regarding choice of articles, size and content of the paper, and treatment of public issues and officials.[24] Although *Red Lion*, and the status of broadcasters generally, was not once mentioned, *Miami Herald* encouraged opponents of broadcast regulation because it rejected claims that the economic-based scarcity of major newspapers justified government intervention. Opponents of the fairness doctrine argued that use of the scarcity rationale by the Court in *Red Lion* was similarly suspect.

---

[20] *Ibid* at 390.
[21] *Ibid* at 390.
[22] *Ibid* at 393.
[23] 412 U.S. 94 (1973).
[24] 418 U.S. 241, 258 (1974).

Ten years later, the Supreme Court, in *FCC v. League of Women Voters*,[25] directly raised the possibility that *Red Lion* would have to be reconsidered, if the fairness doctrine was shown not to enhance speech, or if the scarcity rationale was shown to be invalid. This decision held that the Public Broadcasting Amendments Act, which forbade any "noncommercial educational broadcasting station which receive[d] a grant from the Corporation [for Public Broadcasting] to 'engage in editorializing,'" violated the First Amendment. The Court implied a willingness to revisit *Red Lion* if there was "some signal from Congress or the FCC that technological developments have advanced so far that some revision of the system of broadcast regulations may be required."[26] Although the case did not revolve around the validity of the fairness doctrine, and the relevant comments appeared in two footnotes, the possibility of a reversal suddenly loomed much larger.

Concurrent with these court decisions, the FCC proposed to negate a number of the regulations based on the public trustee standard. Under the stewardship of Chairman Mark Fowler, the FCC in 1981 proposed sweeping deregulation of the broadcasting industry, including abolition of the fairness doctrine and repeal of equal opportunities and reasonable access. Fowler's view was that "the perception of broadcasters as community trustees should be replaced by a view of broadcasters as marketplace participants."[27]

In 1985, following the *League of Women Voters* case, the FCC issued an extensive report concluding that the fairness doctrine no longer served the public interest because it inhibits, rather than encourages, the coverage of controversial issues of public importance. The 1985 FCC report stated that,

> with the potential of government sanction; administrative, legal, and personnel expenses; and reputational costs, there is a significant danger that broadcasters will minimize their presentation of controversial issue programming to avoid the substantial dangers associated with the fairness doctrine.[28]

The Commission argued that because of technological advances and the proliferation of information sources, the fairness doctrine was no longer necessary to assure public access to a variety of viewpoints. As there is an

---

[25] 468 U.S. 364 (1984).

[26] *Ibid* at 376-77 n. 11.

[27] M. Fowler & D. Brenner, *A Marketplace Approach to Broadcast Regulation*, 60 Tex. L. Rev. 207 at 209 (1982).

[28] 1985 Fairness Doctrine Report, 102 FCC 2d 145, 169 (1985).

increase in the number of television and radio stations and the use of new technologies (such as cable television, low power television, and satellite master antenna systems), the public may acquire information about important issues from a wide array of sources. According to the report, "the dynamics of the information services marketplace overall insures that the public will be sufficiently exposed to controversial issues of public importance."[29] The report concluded that since the information the broadcaster provides is no longer unusually scarce or unique, the fairness doctrine should be dropped, and broadcasters should be treated like print journalists.[30]

The FCC's opposition to the fairness doctrine has received the support of most of the broadcast industry, which increasingly argues that stations should be treated just like newspapers and should not be subject to any additional restrictions on free speech.

Industry opposition to the fairness doctrine may be based more on principle than practicality. Henry Geller of the Washington Center for Public Policy Research told the Center, "The entire fight over the fairness doctrine is one of principle. The fairness doctrine doesn't bother them — they're fairer than the fairness doctrine . . . they just don't want you interfering in their business." For similar reasons, the NAB opposes the lowest unit rate "as an unconstitutional infringement on the First Amendment freedoms guaranteed to all in the press, including the broadcast press."[31]

This viewpoint has found support in some of the scholarly literature, which argues that there is no inherent difference between newspapers and electronic media, and that therefore it is unconstitutional to regulate speech on the air to any greater extent than the First Amendment permits regulation of newspapers. Advocates of this position reject scarcity arguments on the grounds that the number of broadcast frequencies could be increased in the future; that the ink, paper and other resources necessary to produce a newspaper are also limited and that daily newspapers are in fact more scarce than television stations. These commentators also point out that no Supreme Court case has endorsed the theory that speech on television can be constitutionally regulated simply because of the power of the medium, anymore than certain daily newspapers can be regulated because of their influence. Although the government owns the airwaves, it has

---

[29] 1985 Fairness Doctrine Report at 197.

[30] Opponents of the doctrine point out that there are actually fewer newspapers than television stations. A single newspaper may be the only newspaper in a city, but that alone does not justify regulation of the content of the newspaper. 1985 Fairness Doctrine Report at 217.

[31] Testimony of Edward O. Fritts, President and CEO of NAB before the House Elections Subcommittee, Committee on House Administration, July 14, 1987, p.3.

no more right to control speech on the air than it does to control speech in a park.[32]

Legal advocates of deregulation place emphasis on the right of the speaker (the station operator) rather than the listener. According to one article co-authored by FCC Commissioner Fowler:

> First, it should be noted that the language of the First Amendment protects the right of speech, not the right of access to ideas or even the right to listen . . . For if listener rights are deemed 'paramount' to broadcaster rights, so the rights of newspaper readers should be paramount to the rights of the publishers and editors and the rights of movie patrons superior to those of exhibitors, distributors, and producers.[33]

These arguments appear to have won some converts in Congress. An aide to one liberal congressman said in the Center's survey: "The airwaves are no longer a 'limited public commodity' but are at present almost limitless or have not been tapped to their limits. Why should we regulate broadcasters when we don't regulate print?"

On the other hand, Congressional supporters of the fairness doctrine argue it is far from clear that the Fairness Doctrine does not accomplish its mission. Referring to the FCC's 1985 report, a 1987 Senate Commerce Committee report stated,

> the failure of the Commission to appreciate that formal and informal use of the Fairness Doctrine has created countless opportunities for expression, as well as its failure to take into account the speech added by uncontested compliance with the doctrine, totally undermines the Commission's conclusion.[34]

---

[32] *See, e.g.,* Lucas A. Powe, Jr, *American Broadcasting and the First Amendment,* University of Calif. Press, 1987, *especially* Ch. 11; See also Matthew Spitzer, *Controlling the Content of Print and Broadcast,* 58 S. Cal. L. Rev. 1349 (1985).

[33] Fowler and Brenner, *A Marketplace Approach to Broadcast Regulation,* pp. 237-38.

[34] Fairness in Broadcasting Act of 1987. Report together with additional and minority views. Senate Committee on Commerce, Science, and Transportation. 100th Cong., 1st Sess., April 3, 1987, p. 23.

It added that past studies had found no "chilling effect," and that few fairness doctrine complaints resulted in FCC action.

The report argued scarcity of information may not be a thing of the past: "scarcity is not a matter of the absolute number of broadcast outlets or new forms of electronic media; as long as more people seek licenses to use the spectrum than can be accommodated, there is scarcity." Although the range of usable broadcast frequencies has been increasing, "the fact remains that demand for broadcast stations far exceeds their availability."[35]

The dramatic increase in amounts paid to purchase a TV license suggests that the licensing process does indeed convey a valuable right because of the relative scarcity of such licensees in the community. During 1985, for example, independent VHF stations were sold for $450 million in Boston, $510 million in Los Angeles, and more than $700 million in New York. In 1987, there were only 10 vacant spectrum spaces, all on UHF channels, in the top 50 media markets.[36]

7. Future Prospects for the Public Trustee Standard

As a result of a constitutional challenge brought by the Meredith Corporation, owner of a television station in Syracuse, NY, the FCC voted unanimously on August 4, 1987 to cease enforcement of the fairness doctrine.[37] In so acting, it overrode the arguments by proponents of the fairness doctrine that Congress had codified the doctrine in the 1959 amendments to the equal opportunities rule, insulating it from administrative repeal by the FCC.[38] The

---

[35] *Ibid* at p. 20.

[36] *Ibid* at pp. 20-21.

[37] In Syracuse Peace Council v. Television Station WTVH, the FCC originally declined to act on the Meredith constitutional challenge, raised when a Fairness Doctrine complaint was brought against the station by the Syracuse Peace Council. But in January 1987, the D.C. Circuit ruled that the Commission was required to address the constitutional question. Meredith Corp. v. FCC, 809 F.2d 863 (D.C. Cir. 1987).

[38] The applicable statutory language is found in 47 U.S.C. 315(a). It reads: "Nothing in the foregoing sentence shall be construed as relieving broadcasters, in connection with the presentation of newscasts, news interviews, and new documentaries, and on-the-spot coverage of news events, from the obligation imposed upon them under this chapter to operate in the public interest and to afford reasonable opportunity for the discussion of conflicting views on issues of public importance." 47 U.S.C. §315(a).

Court in *Red Lion* saw this language as "vindicat[ing] the FCC's general view that the fairness doctrine inhered in the public interest standard."[39] In 1986, the Court of Appeals for the District of Columbia, in an opinion written by Judge Robert Bork, held that the Commission was free to modify the application of the Fairness Doctrine because it is an administrative construct derived from the mandate to serve the public interest, rather than a obligation specified by statute.[40] Public interest organizations petitioned the FCC to reconsider its decision, but a ruling denying that petition was issued on March 24, 1988.

Strong congressional reaction to the Commission's decision and continuing legal challenges have left the future of the fairness doctrine uncertain. Congressional backers of the doctrine in 1987 twice attempted to pass legislation enacting the fairness doctrine into law. In June 1987, the legislation passed the House by a vote of 302 to 102. In the Senate, however, the vote was 59 to 31, less than the two-thirds majority that would have been necessary to override President Reagan's subsequent veto. Fairness doctrine backers then attempted to attach the codifying language to a continuing budget resolution in December 1987, but conferees were forced to remove the provision from the bill when President Reagan threatened to veto the entire continuing resolution over the fairness doctrine issue.

As this monograph goes to press, the FCC decision in the *Meredith* case is still on appeal before the U.S. Court of Appeals. Whatever the court decides, an appeal to the Supreme Court is likely. A final resolution by the courts of the constitutional question may still be several years in the future.

If the Court were to uphold the constitutionality of the fairness doctrine, the validity of basing political broadcasting laws on the public trustee notion would likely be reaffirmed as well. On the other hand, the Court could hold the fairness doctrine unconstitutional either on the grounds that the scarcity on which it rests no longer exists, or on the grounds that it discourages robust debate of controversial issues, instead of promoting it.

In either case, a decision striking down the fairness doctrine on constitutional grounds would also place the current rationale for the regulation of political broadcasting in serious jeopardy; the *Red Lion* opinion closely equates the justification for the equal opportunities rule with the rationale for the fairness doctrine. Though the FCC is arguing in its briefs that only the constitutionality of the fairness doctrine, not the equal opportunities rule, is at issue, the two concepts raise similar factual issues.

---

[39] 395 U.S. at 380

[40] Telecommunications Research & Action Center v. FCC, 801 F.2d 501 (D.C. Cir. 1986).

For example, if the fairness doctrine were held to have a chilling effect on the airing of controversial views, the Court is likely at some future date to reach a similar finding with respect to the equal opportunities rule. Both may encourage a station to avoid presenting candidates or controversial issues in order to avoid having to set aside time for opposing candidates or viewpoints.

A ruling striking down the constitutionality of rules based on the public trustee standard such as the fairness doctrine and equal opportunities would be likely to cause fundamental changes in how the government licenses and regulates the airwaves. But it would not eliminate the right of the government to place conditions on any grant of a broadcasting license. For example, if the government could no longer constitutionally require licensees to comply with the responsibilities of a public trustee, it may decide that the valuable broadcast license should be auctioned off to the highest bidder. Indeed, Rep. John Dingell (D-MI), Chairman of the House Energy and Commerce Committee, has stated that if the fairness doctrine is struck down, "I will work for a new regulatory deal for broadcasting which abandons the public trustee model and looks to spectrum fees or auctions."[41]

In such an auction system, Congress arguably could require any party which bought a broadcast license to comply with certain political broadcasting rules, just as it attaches certain conditions to the sale of other government property, such as offshore drilling rights. Or Congress could impose free media requirements on any licensee by licensing the station to use the airwaves for something less than 24 hours a day, 365 days a year. It would then reserve the remaining time for the use of candidates or other, public service programming. As the court in *Red Lion* points out, the "government could surely have decreed that each frequency should be shared among all or some of those who wish to use it, each being assigned a portion of the broadcast day or the broadcast week."[42] The government could even adjust the price buyers must pay for a station according to the amount of time they agreed to provide candidates.[43]

---

[41] *Television Digest*, March 7, 1988, pp. 1-2, cited in brief of petitioners Henry Geller and Donna Lampert, to the Court of Appeals for the District of Columbia in Syracuse Peace Council v. FCC May 16, 1988, p. 18.

[42] 395 U.S. at 390.

[43] For example, Charles Firestone, adjunct professor of law at UCLA, has proposed an auction system designed to encourage broadcasters to donate public interest time voluntarily. The FCC would auction off broadcast licenses, selling the license at the price the highest bidder would be willing to pay annually for the right to the frequency. The broadcaster could reduce the amount paid the government for the license by the value of time given in public interest or community service programs. For political programming (as well as public service announcements, public access time, and editorial rebuttals) the broadcaster would be allowed to deduct from the annual fee the value of the time,

These policies should not be subject to the same First Amendment objections as the public trustee standard. The airwaves have traditionally been viewed as government property. The Supreme Court has frequently upheld the right of government, like a private owner, to regulate speech on property owned or controlled by the government which is not open to the general public.[44] Since use of the air waves is limited by the government to one licensee, it is, in the terminology of recent Supreme Court cases, a non public forum different from other government property that is used by the general public, such as a park. On two recent occasions the Supreme Court has upheld the right of government to restrict speech in non public governmental forums to certain groups.[45]

Should the government condition purchase of a license on compliance with certain political broadcasting rules, it would be acting in ways less hostile to First Amendment interests than the restrictions upheld in these recent Supreme Court cases. In this case the government would not be regulating the use of its property in a way that limited the speech of some members of the public to the detriment of other members of the public. Instead, it would be conditioning a licensee's use of government property on political broadcasting rules which do not distinguish on the basis of content, which promote equal access rather than deny it, and which are reasonably designed to promote the government's legitimate interests in protecting the integrity of the electoral process.

---

calculated according to the lowest unit rate rules. (Center interview with Charles Firestone, December 29, 1987).

[44] Adderley v. Florida, 385 U.S. 39, 47 (1966) ("The state, no less than a private owner of property, has power to preserve the property under its control for the use to which it is lawfully dedicated.") *See also,* United States Postal Service v. Council of Greenburgh Civic Assns., 453 U.S. 114, 131, fn.7 (1981); Greer v. Spock, 424 U.S. 828, 836 (1976).

[45] Cornelius v. NAACP Legal Defense and Education Fund, 473 U.S. 788 (1985) (federal government may prohibit legal defense and political advocacy groups from participating in government-wide charity drive open to a variety of other charitable organizations); Perry Education Association v. Perry Local Educators' Association, 460 U.S. 37 (1983) (local school board may restrict access to interschool mail system to union certified to represent teachers, while denying access to competing union). A third case upheld against First Amendment challenge the right of a city to prohibit posting of any signs on certain public property. Members of the City Council of Los Angeles v. Taxpayers for Vincent, 466 U.S. 789 (1984). The nature of the air waves as a non public forum would be particularly evident if the Supreme Court struck down the public trustee standard, and the federal government began treating the air wave as a commodity of commercial value appropriately sold to the highest bidder.

Therefore, while the form of licensing and the legal rationale for regulation might differ if the Supreme Court should strike down the public trustee doctrine, the public need in a democracy to regulate candidates' use of the airwaves might well continue to justify government regulation of political broadcasting.

Whether the constitutional basis for such continued regulation is the public trustee standard or some other theory, there would remain practical and policy questions about the content of the political broadcasting requirements imposed on any licensee. The chapters that follow discuss these questions.

4.

Free Media Proposals

My goal is to have as much live discussion as possible. The people need to see the candidates make mistakes, get angry, sweat.

— *A Survey Respondent*

One way to reduce campaign costs and increase the frequency of appearances by candidates on the air is to require broadcasters to provide all candidates a certain amount of time free of charge. While theoretically the time could be provided in any length, including 30- or 60-second spots, most commonly such proposals assume blocks of time at least five minutes long. Such "free media" would be in addition to any coverage of candidates on regularly scheduled news programs or any regularly scheduled news interview programs. Free media may result in stations providing time to candidates to use as they wish, or stations may also choose to retain some editorial control over candidates' use of the time by arranging for the candidates' appearances on special back-to-back news interview programs, debates, or the like. Thus, in this chapter free media means any opportunity (in addition to regularly scheduled news or news interview programs) that a station provides for candidates to appear in segments of five minutes or longer, including time that remains under the editorial control of the station.

Three free media bills introduced in the 100th Congress provided allocations of free broadcast time to House and Senate candidates to use as they wish. Though Congress did not enact any of these bills, the concepts they contain may receive increased attention in the future as substitutes for more comprehensive campaign finance legislation, such as Sen. Robert Byrd's and Sen. Boren's S. 2, which failed to overcome a Republican filibuster on the Senate floor during early 1988.

The purest free media bill in the 100th Congress was Rep. Samuel Stratton's (D-NY) H.R. 521, which would grant major party Senate candidates two hours of free time and major party House candidates one hour of time. Sen. Claiborne Pell's (D-RI) S. 593 and its House companion bill, Rep. Stratton's H.R. 1817, would also grant candidates free time, but would funnel the time through political party committees, which would then allocate the time to candidates. In each bill the stations would be required to provide the time to the candidates without charge, and in segments longer than 60 seconds.

These free media proposals resemble requirements now in place in many other countries. A 1981 American Enterprise Institute study by Anthony Smith found that of 21 democratic countries, 18 of them — all except Norway, Sri Lanka, and the United States — provided free television time to political parties. In 17 countries, free time completely supplanted any paid political advertising. Only Australia, Canada, Japan, and the United States permitted paid advertising.

However, there are a number of substantial economic, political and practical objections to free media which have successfully blocked adoption of the idea. Most broadcasters remain adamantly opposed to the idea. This is not only out of concern with the economic implications of free media, but also because of the practical difficulties broadcasters see with the approach and the precedent it might set for further federal regulation of broadcasting. In addition, members of Congress are likely to view with some skepticism any proposal that might increase their challenger's exposure to the voter.

This chapter examines free media proposals and the objections commonly lodged against them. Based on this analysis, the final section of the chapter contains recommendations for a modified approach to free media.

1. The Politics of Free Media

Free media, if it is to become law, faces two substantial political hurdles: congressional reluctance and broadcaster opposition.

At times in its history, free media has won the support of notable political figures. In connection with congressional consideration in 1970 and 1971 of changes to the political broadcasting laws, Rep. Morris Udall (D-AZ), Rep. Charles Bennett (D-FL), Rep. John Anderson (R-IL), and then California Secretary of State Jerry Brown testified in favor of free media. Another future Congressman who worked in 1971 on behalf of free media was John Anderson's young administrative assistant — David Stockman.

But whatever commitment individual members of Congress may have to free media, some members may be naturally reluctant to alter a political broadcasting system that helped return House members to their seats at a 98 percent reelection rate in 1986.

This concern showed up repeatedly in the Center's survey. While overall reaction to free media was evenly split, challengers were much more enthusiastic about the idea. A total of 60.9 percent of challengers supported requiring broadcasters to provide free time for the use of candidates. Yet only

29.5 percent of incumbents favored this basic form of free media. Democrats were significantly more supportive of free media than were Republicans: 57.3 percent of Democrats as opposed to 34.8 percent of Republicans favored the concept. While support for free media obviously split along lines of partisanship and incumbency, there was little difference between chambers. Of all categories of survey respondents, free media proved most popular among House candidates in the six largest media markets: 68.8 percent of these candidates favored free media. This is probably because high advertising rates in those markets currently restrict those candidates' media exposure.

The chart on the following page summarizes the results of the Center's survey on free media.

Even though public opinion polls have consistently revealed concern about the high costs of political advertising, free media legislation has not generated sustained public interest.[1] Because public support runs wide but shallow, free media proponents in Congress have never been able to turn to grass-roots political pressure to counteract congressional reluctance.

Finally, broadcasters line up unanimously against these proposals. One primary force behind this opposition is the NAB, which considers any free media undesirable. The NAB has attempted to reduce the need for federal regulation by urging its members to voluntarily grant time for debates and other candidate forums. The NAB indicated its aims in a 1986 White Paper, in which it wrote: "by exercising editorial discretion and increasing a station's involvement in the political process, we help to prove to Congress the fallacy of maintaining what are essentially outdated, discriminatory and unconstitutional political broadcasting laws."[2]

Broadcast industry concerns can have a significant impact on Congress. One congressional aide noted that "members fear broadcasters because in areas with only one TV station they can make you or break you." Another veteran of political broadcast reform asserted that "the broadcast lobby is like the highway lobby . . . it's a whole industrial complex. It means newspapers, it means banks, it means advertisers. That's a lot of opposition, and the NAB is capable of putting it all together."

---

[1] A 1983 Harris poll, for example, found 62 percent of the public believed "excessive campaign spending in national elections is a very serious problem"; another 79 percent agreed with the statement, "there ought to be enough free commercial time given to major candidates to allow the voters to get to know them." (The Harris Survey, January 3, 1986 by Louis Harris).

[2] National Association of Broadcasters, "The Role of Broadcasting in the Political Election Process," Washington, D.C., 1986, p. 5.

Views of Survey Respondents on Free Media Proposals

Question:

"Would your candidate favor providing free or discounted time to candidates on radio, television, or cable in one or more of the following ways: Require broadcasters to provide free time for the use of candidates?"

	Overall
Yes	45.4%
No	45.4%
No Opinion	9.2%

	Winners	Losers
Yes	31.9%	60.2%
No	56.0%	33.7%
No Opinion	12.1%	6.0%

	Democrats	Republicans
Yes	57.3%	34.8%
No	35.4%	54.3%
No Opinion	7.3%	10.9%

	House	Senate
Yes	46.4%	41.2%
No	46.4%	41.2%
No Opinion	7.1%	17.6%

	Incumbents	Challengers	Open Seat
Yes	29.5%	60.9%	51.9%
No	57.7%	33.3%	40.7%
No Opinion	12.8%	5.8%	7.4%

By Size of Markets — House only (ADI Rankings)

	1-6	7-25	26-65	66 & up
Yes	68.8%	35.6%	34.5%	50.0%
No	31.3%	60.0%	48.3%	41.2%
No Opinion	0.0%	4.4%	17.2%	8.8%

n = 174

Source: Center for Responsive Politics

2. The Economics of Free Media

Forcing broadcasters to finance media time to federal candidates would clearly result in economic losses to the industry. The extent of these losses, however, is difficult to calculate. Any estimates of free media's actual cost to broadcasters are necessarily tenuous because, as discussed in Chapter Two, the value of air time varies widely from media market to media market, and from program to program.

A New York based study group, the Democracy Project, attempted to make such an assessment in a 1982 report.[3] The report's author, Andrew Buchsbaum, based his cost estimate on a proposal that would grant House candidates a total of 60 minutes of television commercial spots and 60 minutes of program time; Senate candidates would receive 120 minutes of spot time and 90 minutes of program time. One-third of the time would have to appear in prime time and another one-third on weekends. Buchsbaum also allowed candidates to choose free postage over broadcast time.

Buchsbaum estimated the cost of this proposal at $75.9 million per election cycle. Under his proposal, broadcasters would pay half of the broadcast costs — $34 million per two-year period — while the taxpayer would assume the remaining $42 million in broadcast and postage costs.

However, Buchsbaum told the Center he underestimated how much government-financed free spots would cost even then by perhaps 25 percent. In addition, television advertising costs have nearly doubled since 1982. Buchsbaum's proposal, therefore, could cost as much as $200 million per election cycle today. But even if the stations absorbed the entire cost of these forgone advertising revenues, $200 million would still represent less than 1 percent of the TV industry's overall 1986 ad revenues of $22.26 billion.

These amounts represent only the cost of air time, not the cost of production. Media consultant Ed Blakely told the Center that in 1986 the typical 30-second television spot cost $4,000 to produce; the typical radio spot cost $200. The production costs would be higher if free media provided times in periods greater than five minutes. Thirty-minute programs may cost over $100,000 to produce, and for that reason are rarely used today. If free media included debates, which are usually in-studio productions, production costs would be lower. Most free media bills do not specify whether broadcasters would bear the production costs for free media presentations, or whether that responsibility would fall upon the candidates.

---

[3] Andrew Buchsbaum, *Independent Expenditures in Congressional Campaigns: The Electronic Solution*, New York, The Democracy Project (1982).

3. The Issue of Urban Glut

Introduction. Political and economic considerations make free media legislation difficult to pass. There are, however, genuine practical problems as well with any proposal that would grant free time to all candidates. While editorialists perennially express enthusiasm for free media proposals, few have offered constructive suggestions on how they would operate in practice. The main problem that has bedeviled free media is how to provide time for the many races in large markets, such as New York and Los Angeles, without swamping local broadcasters. For example, when The Twentieth Century Fund's Commission on Campaign Costs in the Electronic Era, led by former FCC chairman Newton N. Minow, issued its 1969 report entitled *Voter's Time*, proposing free media, the commission confined its study to presidential elections. It did not address the "urban candidate glut" problems that arise from House races.[4] A 1983 article advocating free media noted, "nobody has ever come up with a workable formula about how to allot free time, especially for Congressional races...."[5]

In the past, these practical difficulties have played a prominent role in congressional consideration of free media bills. During debates on changes to the political broadcasting laws between 1969 to 1971, each formula for allocating free time came under attack as impractical and discriminatory. Free media opponents saw urban glut as a supposedly insoluble problem. Proposals in the recent past have met a similar reaction. However, Senator Robert Dole once commented, "If they can figure out the tax code, they can figure this (free media) out."[6]

The Diagnosis. The Twentieth Century Fund, in its follow-up to the *Voter's Time* report, identified the urban glut problem:

> Television campaigning is not suited to many districts. The forty or so congressional districts in the New York prime viewing area create a real problem for any free time proposal. Would the 11 television stations in New York be forced to

---

[4] *Voter's Time: Report of the Twentieth Century Fund Commission on Campaign Costs in the Electronic Era*, the Twentieth Century Fund, N.Y., 1969.

[5] Neil Hickey, "A Call for Reform: Less Convention Coverage, More Presidential Debates, Free Political Commercials," *TV Guide*, October 1, 1983, p. 40.

[6] Elizabeth Drew, *Politics and Money*, New York, Macmillan Co., 1983, p. 151.

> provide free time to all the New York and nearby Connecticut and New Jersey candidates?[7]

Network executives have often expressed extreme discomfort over such a thought:

> It would mean an end to regular programming ... jeopardize programming for the networks themselves and possibly deny programs to the rest of the country ... It would mean an unending stream of political messages that would be calculated to turn off television sets as effectively as a power failure in the New York area.[8]

Whether or not free media would lead to such disastrous outcomes, it would clearly place a heavy load on the shoulders of broadcasters in major markets. This was detailed most graphically by Roger D. Colloff, now General Manager of WCBS-TV in New York:

> ... a requirement that broadcasters provide even one half-hour of free time to each of these federal candidates would have compelled WCBS-TV to present a total of 99 hours of free political programming prime time — almost 3 hours a night — during the 35 consecutive nights preceding the 1980 election. The resulting burden on the station would have been crippling, entailing an enormous revenue loss and the virtual total preemption of all other prime time programming. And what would have been the compensating gain for the political process? What portion of the normal prime time audience could be expected to sit through a steady diet of back-to-back political speeches, many of which would be from Congressional candidates whose districts comprised only a tiny fraction of the station's viewership? ... Gubernatorial, mayoral, and other non-federal candidates could well find themselves relegated to undesirable time periods,

---

[7] David Rosenbloom, *Electing Congress*, New York, The Twentieth Century Fund, p. 78.

[8] Testimony of ABC Vice President Everett H. Erlich, Hearings on H.R. 7612, Committee on House Administration, 1973, p. 89.

or unable to purchase time at all on stations already deluged with free political programming for federal candidates.[9]

A Curable Problem. Any realistic free media proposal must address the urban glut problem. But urban glut need not ring the death knell for free media. First, it should be noted that the problem only exists in a handful of markets. The charts on the following pages indicate that in only six metropolitan areas — New York, Los Angeles, Chicago, Philadelphia, Boston, and Detroit — is the media market the primary market for ten or more House districts. In only three other markets — San Francisco, Cleveland, and Atlanta — are there even as many as seven congressional districts within the primary media market or "Area of Dominant Influence"(ADI). The urban glut problem is therefore largely contained within these nine markets, which encompass 30 percent of the nation's congressional districts.

One solution to urban candidate glut, therefore, would be to put a ceiling on the amount of total free time each station would be required to provide. This approach might not permit coverage of all races in the largest markets. But it assumes that the public interest is better served by providing time for *some* candidates, instead of forgoing free media altogether because of the practical difficulties in providing time for *all*.

Under this proposal, no television or radio station would have to carry more than a certain number of minutes of free time. Stations could meet before the campaign and divide responsibility for the races among themselves either by lottery or by negotiations. A particular television station might assume responsibility for three specific races, for instance, leaving other races for other stations. As an alternative, each station, acting alone, could exercise its own editorial discretion in deciding which races should receive the free time. Once a station provided free time to one candidate, of course, it would have to provide an equal amount of free time to all major opponents of that candidate in the same race.

This approach is not without pitfalls. All of the broadcasters in a market might provide free time only for the most heated races, or the races with the most colorful candidates, leaving other races uncovered. If a large proportion of the races in a market received no air time, one of the purposes of free media — leveling the playing field for *all* candidates — would be undermined.

---

[9] Testimony of Roger D. Colloff, then Vice President, Policy and Planning, CBS/Broadcast Group, Hearings before the Senate Rules and Administration Committee, Sept. 29, 1983, p. 462.

Comparison of Congressional Districts and Media Markets

	ADI	# of CDs In Primary Media Market	# of CDs In Secondary Media Market	#of VHF Stations	#of UHF Stations	#of CDs per VHF Stations in Primary Market
1)	New York	33	7	7	13	4.7
2)	Los Angeles	21	1	7	10	3.0
3)	Chicago	16	1	5	14	3.2
4)	Philadelphia	13	9	4	15	3.3
5)	San Francisco	9	2	7	16	1.3
6)	Boston	12	1	5	14	2.4
7)	Detroit	11	1	4	7	2.8
8)	Dallas-Ft.Worth	6	1	5	6	1.0
9)	Washington, DC	5	2	4	12	1.3
10)	Houston	6	2	4	6	1.0
11)	Cleveland	8	0	3	12	2.7
12)	Atlanta	7	1	4	6	1.8
13)	Pittsburgh	5	3	3	7	1.7
14)	Miami	5	1	7	7	0.7
15)	Minneapolis/St.Paul	4	3	6	6	0.7
16)	Seattle-Tacoma	6	0	7	8	0.9
17)	Tampa-St. Petersburg	4	0	4	6	1.0
18)	St. Louis	5	3	5	2	1.0
19)	Denver	5	1	9	5	0.6
20)	Sacramento-Stockton	2	4	4	6	0.5
21)	Baltimore	4	1	3	5	1.3
22)	Phoenix	5	0	7	4	1.3

Continued on next page

Comparison of Congressional Districts and Media Markets *(continued)*

	ADI	# of CDs In Primary Media Market	# of CDs In Secondary Media Market	#of VHF Stations	#of UHF Stations	#of CDs per VHF Stations in Primary Market
23)	Hartford-New Haven	5	0	2	9	2.5
24)	Indianapolis	4	3	4	7	1.0
25)	San Diego	3	1	3	4	1.0
26)	Portland	5	3	7	4	0.7
27)	Orlando-Daytona Beach-Melbourne	2	3	3	10	0.7
28)	Cincinnati	3	2	3	7	1.0
29)	Kansas City	2	2	4	5	0.5
30)	Milwaukee	3	1	4	7	0.8
31)	Nashville	2	3	4	6	0.5
32)	Charlotte	3	1	2	7	1.5
33)	New Orleans	2	1	4	4	0.5
34)	Columbus	6	5	3	4	2.0
35)	Raleigh-Durham	2	1	3	7	0.7
36)	Buffalo	5	0	3	5	1.7
37)	Oklahoma City	3	1	5	8	0.6
38)	Greenville-Spartansburg-Asheville	1	0	3	11	0.3
39)	Memphis	3	1	4	3	0.8
40)	Grand Rapids-Kalamazoo-Battle Creek	3	1	3	6	1.0
41)	Salt Lake City	2	4	9	4	0.2

Continued on next page

Comparison of Congressional Districts and Media Markets *(continued)*

	ADI	# of CDs In Primary Media Market	# of CDs In Secondary Media Market	#of VHF Stations	#of UHF Stations	#of CDs per VHF Stations in Primary Market
42)	Providence-New Bedford	2	4	3	5	0.7
43)	Birmingham	4	0	4	5	1.0
44)	San Antonio	2	2	4	4	0.5
45)	Harrisburg-York-Lancaster-Lebanon	2	0	1	7	2.0
46)	Norfolk-Portsmouth-Newport News	3	0	3	5	1.0
47)	Charleston-Huntington	1	0	3	9	0.3
48)	Dayton	2	1	2	5	1.0
49)	Louisville	3	1	2	6	1.5
50)	Greensboro-Winston-Salem-High Point	2	0	3	6	0.7
51)	Albany-Schenectady-Troy	4	0	3	6	1.3
52)	Tulsa	2	0	5	6	0.4
53)	Little Rock	2	2	6	5	0.3
54)	West Palm Beach-Ft. Pierce-Vero Beach	2	1	2	5	1.0
55)	Mobile-Pensacola	1	1	3	9	0.3
56)	Flint-Saginaw-Bay City	2	2	2	8	1.0
57)	Jacksonville	2	3	4	3	0.5
58)	Wichita-Hutchinson	1	2	12	2	0.1
59)	Wilkes-Barre-Scranton	3	0	0	7	—

Continued on next page

Comparison of Congressional Districts and Media Markets (continued)

	ADI	# of CDs In Primary Media Market	# of CDs In Secondary Media Market	#of VHF Stations	#of UHF Stations	#of CDs per VHF Stations in Primary Market
60)	Richmond	2	1	3	6	0.7
61)	Knoxville	3	1	3	3	1.0
62)	Shreveport-Texarkana	2	0	3	4	0.7
63)	Fresno-Visalia	3	0	0	10	—
64)	Toledo	3	1	2	4	1.5
65)	Albuquerque	3	0	9	5	0.3

Notes

ADI: The Area of Dominant Influence. Counties are assigned to an ADI according to which stations are most heavily viewed in that county; each county is assigned to only one ADI.

Primary media market: The TV market which corresponds to the largest portion of a particular congressional district.

Secondary media market: In some cases, a second ADI covers a lesser portion of the congressional district. For example, Connecticut's Third District, which is primarily covered by the Hartford-New Haven TV market, is also served by New York stations. In this case, New York would be considered a "secondary" market.

VHF: The number of stations on the frequency covering channels 2-13 in the given ADI.

UHF: The number of stations from channels 14-83 in the given ADI.

CD: Congressional District. To provide a rough estimate of the potential for urban glut in each market, this column reflects the ratio of the number of congressional districts per VHF station in the primary market. VHF stations are the ones most likely to reach all portions of each ADI.

Source: Center for Responsive Politics

On the other hand, with full cooperation among all the stations, candidates in most races would have the opportunity to appear in at least one half-hour program. For example, in New York, if each of the 20 UHF or VHF stations in the New York ADI devoted a half-hour program to each of four separate races, this would provide coverage of 80 congressional races, twice the 40 congressional districts that are part of the New York media market.

Of all the alternatives that would circumvent the urban glut problem, the respondents to the Center's survey preferred permitting broadcasters to allocate the air time among themselves. The results are summarized in the chart on the following page. Overall, 50.6 percent of respondents supported this approach. It enjoyed considerable support among winners as well as losers. Further analysis of the data by the Center indicated that, in fact, support among incumbents (50.7 percent) was almost equal to support among challengers (54.4 percent). The responses indicate that imposing free media requirements on a per-station rather than per-candidate basis provides one politically acceptable way to craft a free media proposal that avoids the urban glut problem.

An alternative cure for urban glut is to funnel free media through the House and Senate campaign committees of each party. Sen. Pell's bill, for example, would grant up to three hours of free television time per station to the committees; the committees would then allocate that time to the party's candidates. Thus, no station would need to provide more than 12 hours of time (three hours to the House and Senate campaign committees of each party) during the 60 days before an election. In effect, under this proposal the parties rather than the broadcaster would decide which races should receive coverage, and in what amounts.

In allocating their time, the party campaign committees would presumably grant more time to candidates who would benefit most from the exposure — those in tight races. Another possibility, suggested by University of Virginia political scientist Larry Sabato, is that parties might "air generic institutional advertising in the large media markets — crowding all candidates under the party umbrella without special attention to any one."[10]

The Pell proposal successfully avoids urban glut by requiring parties rather than broadcasters to choose among a large number of races. It would also have the effect of boosting the influence of parties in congressional elections, and increasing the ability of the party to influence members on legislative matters in Congress. If the party controlled the ability of incumbents to appear on the air, members would be more likely to follow the legislative lead of the party leadership. According to Pell aide Orlando Potter, the impact of the

---

[10] Sabato, *The Party's Just Begun*, p. 220.

Views of Survey Respondents on Proposals to Avoid Urban Glut

"Would you permit broadcasters to allocate the air time of candidates among themselves, so that no one station has to provide time for all the races?"

	Overall	Winners	Losers
Yes	50.6%	43.5%	58.0%
No	33.7%	35.3%	32.1%
No Opinion	15.7%	21.2%	9.9%

n = 166

"Would you require the broadcasters to give the free time to the House and Senate campaign committees of both national political parties (rather than candidates themselves) to allocate among candidates as they decide?"

	Overall	Winners	Losers
Yes	22.5%	25.0%	19.8%
No	63.3%	55.7%	71.6%
No Opinion	14.2%	19.3%	8.6%

n = 169

"Would you require the FCC to allocate the free time among the stations, so that no one station has to provide time for all of the candidates?"

	Overall	Winners	Losers
Yes	49.7%	37.2%	63.0%
No	34.7%	41.9%	27.2%
No Opinion	15.6%	20.9%	9.9%

n = 167

"Would you provide postage or newspaper advertising subsidies as an alternative to free air time for candidates?"

	Overall	Winners	Losers
Yes	29.5%	14.1%	45.7%
No	56.6%	64.7%	48.1%
No Opinion	13.9%	21.2%	6.2%

n= 166

Source: Center for Responsive Politics

bill on the influence of the party was an important motivation for utilizing the campaign committees.

The historian Arthur M. Schlesinger, Jr. has also advocated giving parties free TV time so as to enhance the influence of the parties, while reducing the cost of campaigns.[11]

The chief advantage of this approach may be its chief disadvantage as well. In essence, the Pell bill superimposes a European, party-oriented political broadcasting system on this country's candidate-oriented electoral system. By giving power to allocate time to party committees headed by incumbents, the committees may unfairly favor incumbents over challengers, or party elders over junior members. Maverick candidates outside the party establishment might receive less time. Because each party would receive separate allocations, there might also be fewer joint appearances by opposing candidates than if the stations controlled the time.

The Pell proposal was very unpopular among candidates in the Center's survey. Only 22.5 percent (against 63.3 percent opposed) supported allocating free time through the House and Senate campaign committees. Particularly vehement in their opposition to this proposal were challengers (14.7 percent supported, 73.5 percent opposed), many of whom indicated in their survey responses that they felt they received less support than incumbents from their party's congressional campaign committees in 1986. One losing senatorial candidate complained to the Center, "Campaign committee staffs are a bunch of liars."

Even some victorious candidates were skeptical about granting broadcast time to the campaign committees. One junior House member said, "Incumbents will talk to their buddies and they'll be the ones who get time."

Allowing campaign committees or broadcast stations to allocate free time is not the only way to avoid urban glut. For example, Congress could sidestep the problem altogether by exempting stations in the top six media markets from providing any free media time. Alternatively, it could limit free media just to Senate races — the races which rely most heavily on broadcasting and pose few logistical problems in allocating time because the number of races is limited as a general matter to one per state.

---

[11] Arthur M. Schlesinger, Jr., *The Cycles of American History,* Houghton Miffin Co., Boston, 1986, p. 270. "America is almost alone among the Atlantic democracies in declining to provide political parties free prime time on television during elections. Were the United States to follow the civilized example, it could do much both to bring inordinate campaign costs under control and to revitalize the political parties."

However, restricting free media in this manner undermines the goal of improving media access for as many candidates as possible. Excluding stations in the largest media markets from general free media obligations would run counter to the principle that all stations have responsibilities as public trustees. If only Senate candidates were granted free media time, House candidates in the largest markets would continue to be largely invisible. Senate candidates, who can generally afford advertising already, would receive even more airtime.

4. Scheduling Questions

Effect on Station's Regular Programming. Besides urban candidate glut, broadcasters typically object that free media presentations of longer than commercial length will disrupt their schedules and force them to edit their programs drastically. For example, if Congress decided that five-minute presentations were an ideal length, broadcasters would have to carve out five-minute slots from a schedule constructed in half-hour blocks. Sen. Pell's S. 593 provided for free media presentations of between one and fifteen minutes in length, but does not specify how long they should be, or who should decide upon the length. If broadcasters only presented one 15-minute program, or granted two five-minute presentations, they would either have to find filler programming for the remainder of the half-hour, or else heavily edit the scheduled program.

The networks have, on several occasions, shortened their programs by five minutes in order to accept political ads from presidential candidates. But doing so frequently could undermine public support for free media. Postponements and changes of favorite television programs often trigger loud public outcries. As one respondent to the Center's survey put it, "Nobody wants to see local candidates when a favorite program is on. People don't want to miss 'Cagney and Lacey.'"

Furthermore, scheduling disruptions undermine the delicate relationship between networks and their affiliate stations. Because a network depends upon affiliates consistently running its programs, it is not likely to tolerate an affiliate which regularly preempts its programming, or even cuts network programs by five minutes.

In order to reduce these problems and maximize the audience for free media presentations, some free media legislation has proposed ways to institutionalize a time for such presentations. Sen. Pell's bill specifies all free media spots would air during the "prime time access period."[12] The FCC set aside this period in 1970 for creative local programming, but it has instead become the preserve of syndicated programming such as "Wheel of Fortune" and "Entertainment Tonight." By limiting all presentations to prime time access, Pell would minimize disruptions in broadcast schedules, and place political broadcasts in a regular time slot to which viewers can become accustomed.

Broadcasters could also institutionalize a time slot and avoid editing quandaries by placing all or most free media presentations immediately after local newscasts, which most television stations run at least once a day. Because newscasts generally last 30 or 60 minutes, and may be more easily shortened, a loss of five minutes at the end of a local newscast would reduce viewers' complaints. Indeed, stations today commonly shorten these newscasts in order to offer editorials and editorial rebuttals. However, this approach would primarily reach those who are already information-hungry (not the less informed voters whom political advertising can reach effectively). The audience also would be somewhat smaller than in prime time, or the prime time access period.

Simultaneity. In order to assure that appearances which are made possible by free media requirements reach the widest possible audience, some proposals have required that all broadcast stations in a market simultaneously carry presentations of political candidates. Under simultaneity, at a particular time (e.g., 7:30 p.m. on the Mondays during the election period), every station in the media market would be required to feature some race, although not necessarily the same one.

Some believe simultaneity represents one way to combine the often irreconcilable goals of raising the quality of political debate, and of controlling campaign costs. Free media can only substitute for paid advertisements if the messages reach the uninformed and undecided voters that 30-second ads target. Without simultaneity, voters uninterested in the political process will likely switch to another program during free media time. With simultaneity, candidates would reach a greater proportion of voters.

Simultaneity has been a part of free media proposals for a number of years. The Twentieth Century Fund Commission's *Voter's Time* report, which stemmed from its concern over the growing use of advertisements in campaigns and its desire to promote "rational political discussions," included simultaneity as a key part of its proposal for free time in presidential elections. Under the proposal, every television and radio station in the U.S. would have been required to broadcast *Voter's Time* presentations simultaneously. Simultaneity was

---

[12] Week night and Saturday prime time access hours in most markets are, in the Eastern and Western time zones, 7:00-8:00 p.m., and in the Central and Mountain time zones, 6:00-7:00 p.m.

crucial, the Commission felt, to allow Americans to "sit down together to watch, listen, and make judgments about the men who would lead them."[13]

Disputing the assertion that simultaneity would drive viewers to turn off their sets *en masse*, the Twentieth Century Fund's Commission maintained that the British experience with campaign party broadcasts indicates little drop-off in viewership. Because it breaks from normal TV fare, simultaneity would impress upon the American people the importance of the campaign process. The Commission, dismissing arguments that simultaneity was similar to the inescapable presence of Orwell's "Big Brother," noted that viewers would be under no compulsion to watch television at all during the time the candidates appeared.

While the *Voter's Time* report only addressed presidential elections, it influenced free media proposals for congressional elections, as well. For example, the bill Reps. John B. Anderson and Morris K. Udall introduced in 1971 to provide "Voter's Time" to congressional candidates included the concept of simultaneity. It allocated two publicly financed half-hour blocks to major party House candidates and three blocks to Senate candidates, with lesser allocations for minor party candidates. The bill specified that "Voter's Time" broadcasts would only appear at one time per evening in each media market. Different candidates could appear on different channels, allowing viewers to choose the channel on which candidates from their own district were appearing.

Of the bills in the 100th Congress, only Rep. Stratton's H.R. 521 incorporated simultaneity. Under the proposal, major party Senate candidates would receive two hours of broadcast time that must be carried simultaneously by all television stations within the state, as well as out-of-state stations which serve the state. Stratton included no such simultaneity requirement for House elections.

The idea of simultaneity incurs the strong opposition of broadcasters, who see it as a serious infringement of their editorial independence. Ward Chamberlin, president of public broadcast station WETA-TV told the Center:

> Requiring all stations to do something at a certain time cuts against the grain of any broadcaster's instincts . . . I wouldn't mind a requirement that public television carry a certain amount of material, but I don't want the federal government to tell me I have to put on a specific program at a specific time.

---

[13] *Voter's Time: Report of the Twentieth Century Fund Commission on Campaign Costs in the Electronic Era*, the Twentieth Century Fund, N.Y., p. 33.

Some broadcasters argue simultaneity would not achieve its goals. Video cassette recorders would permit viewers to avoid political broadcasts by watching taped programs. National cable services, which could not be included under any single market's simultaneity requirement for congressional races, would give many viewers another recourse. Or, people on those nights might decide to do something other than watch television.

The Center tested support for simultaneity in its survey, asking whether respondents would support requiring broadcasters to "at least set aside a specific day before the election when all stations would have to simultaneously provide time to various candidates." Simultaneity enjoyed less support in the survey than did other free media options: only 27.6 percent of respondents (and only 11.7 percent of incumbents) favored this simultaneity proposal, while 58.2 percent opposed it.

5. Third Parties and Free Media

Any free media proposal must consider how to treat third party candidates. On the one hand, free media legislation should contain some provisions that would allow third parties, particularly emerging parties with significant public support, to obtain free broadcast time. Clearly, the communications law should not discriminate against strong third parties such as the Populists in the 1890's, the Bull Moose Party in 1912, and George Wallace's American Independent Party in 1968. On the other hand, if parties with negligible public support, such as the Vegetarian Party or the "Down with Lawyers" Party (a party which placed a presidential candidate on the ballot in New Jersey in 1980) are included, the urban glut problem would be compounded and the airwaves would be filled by fringe parties of little or no general interest. The balance must rest somewhere in between.

The Center's survey revealed a strong sentiment for granting some free time to third party candidates. Of those polled, 62.5 percent favored providing free or discounted time to third party candidates. Among incumbents, 52.7 percent supported this proposition, and among challengers 77.6 percent supported granting free time to third parties.

Free media bills in the 100th Congress addressed the third party question in divergent ways.

Rep. Andrew Jacobs (D-IN) introduced H.R. 480, a bill which grants publicly financed free time, would provide government-funded free time to all candidates on the ballot, even fringe candidates. This approach would exacerbate the urban glut problem. Not only would every major party candidate receive the full allotment of time, but also any fringe candidate who jumps into the race in order to take advantage of the free media time.

Rep. Stratton's H.R. 521 took a different approach, granting parties different amounts of time depending on their strength. Stratton defines three categories of candidates: 1) "major party," any party whose candidate placed first or second in either of the most recent elections; 2) "third party," any party whose candidate received more than 15 percent of the vote in the most recent election; and 3) "minor party," any party whose candidate received more than 5 percent of the vote or who can obtain petition signatures of 5 percent of the state or district's registered voters (to provide a means for new or emerging parties to qualify for time).

The Stratton bill allocated different time to candidates depending on these categories. Major party Senate candidates receive two hours of time, third party candidates receive one hour, and minor party candidates get 30 minutes. House candidates in the three categories receive one hour, fifteen minutes, and fifteen minutes. Candidates below the 5 percent threshold receive no time.

Sen. Pell's bill grants the full free time allocation to any party that finished above 5 percent in the last election, or can obtain signatures of 5 percent of the voters. Candidates below this level receive no time, as in the Stratton bill.

Both proposals allow strong minor parties adequate air time and, through the petition mechanism, provide media time for the new, emerging party. As demonstrated by the charts on third parties appearing in Chapter Seven, few third parties have exceeded the 5 percent level in congressional elections, with the exception of state-specific parties such as the New York Liberal and Conservative parties.

There is precedent in the campaign laws for distinguishing between major party candidates and third party candidates. Public funding of presidential candidates only applies to those candidates whose parties received greater than 5 percent of the vote in the previous election.[14] In 1976 the Supreme Court upheld in *Buckley v. Valeo* the constitutionality of the public funding provisions of the Federal Election Campaign Act against a claim that they violated the equal protection clause, applicable to the federal government under the Fifth Amendment.[15] The Court held that the public financing provisions were enacted to further sufficiently important governmental interests, and

---

[14] 26 U.S.C. 9004.
[15] 424 U.S. 1 (1976).

furthermore, that the law did not unfairly or unnecessarily burden the political opportunity of any minor party or candidate.[16]

6. Primaries and Free Media

If urban candidate glut confounds broadcasters in general elections, in which only one candidate per party runs for each office, it threatens to swamp them if all primary candidates were to receive equal time. Even though in some states and districts it is the primary, not the general election, that creates the most heated races, none of the free media bills in the 100th Congress applied to primary elections.

In allocating free media time during primaries, the per station requirement does not work very effectively. If the stations were allowed to choose which party's primaries to feature, broadcasters might unfairly favor one party over the other. But forcing them to grant *equal* time to both parties' races would be equally inappropriate since very few House races have competitive primaries in both parties. In other cases, the number of candidates in particular primaries might create unavoidable urban glut problems for the station left with no option but to present all the candidates in the primary for the party's nomination, including all the fringe candidates.

Using the Pell party committee allocation system also does not work as successfully for primaries as for general elections. Since Pell's proposal would give the party complete control over which contenders received air time, discrimination against outsiders could be heightened. The party itself would, in essence, be choosing among its own candidates before any votes are cast.

7. Government Financing of Free Media

While all of the proposals discussed so far would require stations to provide time to candidates free of charge, other free media proposals provide government funds to reimburse broadcasters for the time. This approach has two major advantages. It substantially reduces objections against forcing broadcasters

---

[16] *Ibid* at pp. 95-96. The Court observed that the public financing provisions would not prevent any candidate from getting on the ballot, or any voter from casting a vote for the candidate of his choice. Minor party candidates' inability, if any, to wage effective campaigns derives not from lack of public funding, but from their inability to raise private contributions. The Court discussed the fact that major party candidates voluntarily received such funding in exchange for agreeing to restrict their own expenditures, whereas minor party candidates who receive no public financing have no such expenditures limits. However, the Court did not rely solely on this fact in upholding the Act against equal protection arguments.

to bear the cost of the candidates' campaigns, and it creates additional ways to resolve the urban glut problem. Broadcasters could no longer complain of discrimination. However, because this approach amounts, in effect, to partial public financing of congressional elections, it brings with it all the political difficulties inherent in any public campaign financing proposal.

The bill introduced by Rep. Andrew Jacobs, H.R. 480, is the only legislation in the 100th Congress which proposed free media financed by the government. It would provide to each candidate government funds to purchase 90 minutes of television time, with each appearance at least five minutes long; 135 minutes of radio time; and 126 column inches of newspaper advertising (or one page, whichever is greater). Candidates would also receive an allotment of funds to cover the costs of installation of phones and other equipment for question-and-answer programs on television and radio. Jacobs told the Center that since "campaigning is the communication of ideas," government financing for communications media alone would meet candidates' needs sufficiently.

In 1969, the *Voter's Time* report also argued that any free media time should be publicly (government) financed: "Since we believe that 'Voter's Time' is public time, serving all the people, we hold that the public should pay for it."[17]

Government financing of free media could also facilitate a solution to the urban candidate glut problem. If the government pays for the media time, it can provide alternative benefits — such as postage discounts — as a substitute for candidates for whom television is inefficient. For example, each qualifying House candidate could receive a voucher worth a uniform amount of dollars, based on the value of a specific amount of prime time in an average media market. Candidates could choose to spend their voucher either on television advertising or on radio, cable, or postage during the 60 days before an election, depending on which was most cost-effective in that market.[18] Those in the most

---

[17] *Voter's Time: Report of the Twentieth Century Fund Commission on Campaign Costs in the Electronic Era*, p. 28. Others, such as Herbert Alexander of the Citizens Research Foundation suggest broadcasters and taxpayers share the costs. The 1982 Democracy Project report proposed splitting costs equally and suggested allocating the surplus money from the presidential election checkoff fund — about $13 million a year — to cover the government's portion of the cost.

[18] Two pieces of legislation in the 100th Congress proposed postage subsidies for candidates: Rep. Swift's H.R. 2464, a discounted advertising/campaign spending limitation bill; and the Byrd-Boren public financing/spending limitation bill (S. 2). Both bills thus use postage discounts merely as an additional inducement for *all* candidates to accept spending limitations, not as a solution to the urban glut problem or as part of a free media proposal. *(cont'd)*

expensive media markets, where the urban glut problem exists, would be more likely to choose postage over broadcasting.

The Center's survey indicates that many candidates under such a program would in fact choose postage grants as an alternative to free broadcast time. In response to the question, "During the 1986 campaign, on which type of communications did your campaign spend the most money," 53.1 percent of House candidates in the nation's six largest media markets said they relied most heavily on direct mail, with radio finishing a distant second at 18.8 percent.

Even in smaller markets, candidates make substantial use of direct mail: in markets ranked 7th through 25th and 26th through 65th in the nation, direct mail was the top choice of over 20 percent of candidates, second to only commercial television.

While publicly financed media time seems workable and might overcome broadcaster opposition, general public financing schemes have continually bumped up against the unwillingness of Congress to use government funds to finance campaigns. As political consultant Frank Greer told the Center: "The American public wants to do something about campaign finance reform and they want to limit the cost of campaigning. But when you tell them that the real way to make it fair is to pass public financing, they say, 'Hold on, I don't want these politicians spending *my* money.'"

Others object to spending public money on broadcasters who, according to this argument, should provide the time free. In 1969, Nicholas Johnson, then a commissioner at the FCC, questioned the Twentieth Century Fund Commission's recommendation that *Voter's Time* be publicly financed: "an industry that is using public property, the airwaves," should not "hold up the elected public officials and make them pay to get time from public property." [19] Political consultant Robert Squier in an interview with the Center carried this critique one step further, calling publicly financed media time a "double tax" that forces the public to pay for reclaiming public property.

---

18 *(cont'd)* Currently, Congress only appropriates money to subsidize the one postage class that operates at a loss, bulk mail for non-profit organizations. The Democracy Project report also proposed offering all candidates a choice between free broadcast time and enough free postage "...to mail to every potential voter in their district" (Buchsbaum, p. 112). But because the proposal would provide the same amount of TV time for all candidates and grant postal subsidies equal to the value of the forgone TV time, it would not create much incentive for urban candidates to accept postage rather than television time.

[19] *The New York Times*, Oct. 12, 1969.

The Center's survey found strong opposition to free media financed by the government. Only 16.4 percent of respondents (and only 8.0 percent of incumbents) supported having the federal government pay the cost of broadcast time for candidates. Several respondents, including some who supported free media, mentioned their opposition to public financing during the survey's open-ended questions. As one put it, "Because the license to broadcast is issued by the federal government, it should be the responsibility of broadcasters . . . the government should not pay for the time."

Respondents to the Center's survey also strongly opposed providing postage subsidies (or newspaper advertising subsidies) for candidates as an alternative to free air time. Overall, 29.5 percent favored this proposal, with 56.6 percent opposed, and 13.9 percent expressing no opinion; among incumbents, only 16.7 percent favored postage subsidies, with 61.1 percent opposed, and 22.2 percent expressing no opinion.

This may be because incumbent members of Congress do not want to enhance challengers' access to voters' mailboxes. Self-generated output (mail other than that responding to constituents' correspondence) accounts for some 92 percent of congressional mail and the volume and cost of outgoing mail are especially high during election years.[20] In 1982, for example, the cost and volume of congressional mail almost doubled from 1981 levels.

8. Recommendations

The details of a free media approach can be crafted in many different ways; the following proposal illustrates one kind of free media requirement that could improve the electoral process without overburdening broadcasters:

- During every general election period each television station in the nation should be required to provide, in addition to its regular news programming, four half-hour programs on House races and four additional half-hour programs if the market serves a state which has a Senate race. To maximize the audience, all programs would appear simultaneously on specific nights of the week during the prime time access period (e.g. 7:30 p.m. to 8:00 p.m.). To assure that the presentations have maximum impact, all programs would appear during the four weeks prior to the general election. Time would be equally divided among the major candidates, in blocks of at least five minutes in length.

---

[20] *Congressional Quarterly*, Oct. 19, 1985, p. 2109.

- The stations could provide the time to the candidates to use as they wish, or they could keep control of the format themselves and produce debates or other, innovative formats featuring the candidates.

- To avoid urban candidate glut in House elections, broadcasters could choose the races that receive free time.

- For both the House and Senate, all candidates whose party obtained at least 5 percent of the vote in the previous election for the same office, or who can obtain petition signatures of 5 percent of those registered to vote in the pending election, would receive time equal to the major parties.

The Center believes that free media proposals remain the most direct way to ensure that the electorate has ample opportunities to observe the candidates and assess their qualifications. Free media, presupposing as it does more substantive appearances by candidates of at least five minutes in duration, remains a healthy antidote to an over reliance on the 30- second spot. As discussed in Chapter Two, short, 30- or 60-second commercials may help inform a certain segment of the populace. But Americans feel uneasy about the increasing number of such commercials because they run counter to our democratic ideals, symbolized by town meetings, debates between candidates, and grass-roots political activity.

While survey respondents overall split evenly on the general proposal that stations provide free time to candidates, the proposal drew substantial support from challengers (60.9 percent), Democrats (57.3 percent), and candidates for the House from the six largest media markets (68.8 percent).

In the past, free media proposals have been defeated in part by arguments that urban candidate glut and other practical problems make the concept unworkable. This need not be so. A reasonable solution to the urban glut problem is to mandate that each *station* provide a certain amount of free time for candidates, rather than to grant each *candidate* a certain amount of free air time. While this approach would not give every candidate in every congressional race equal amounts of free air time, the requirement would improve access to the airwaves for most candidates.

In large urban centers, stations would exercise their news judgment in deciding which races should receive free time. No single station would be required to provide more than four hours of free time, assuming a Senate as well as House race in the market served. Urban stations would not face any greater burden than a station in a much smaller media market.

Authorizing the stations rather than the candidates to determine the format of the candidate's appearance addresses criticisms that candidates may abuse the free time privilege and produce uninformative or dull programming. As opposed to allowing the FCC or the congressional campaign committees to allocate time, the broadcast stations themselves are the most logical choice to determine the format of the presentations. They are close to the races, they possess the equipment and on-air talent, and they have an interest in making the presentations compelling. The station would preserve the option to feature just one race during its half-hour, or to feature up to three separate races in shorter segments.

Under the Center's proposal, broadcasters would face only minimal economic loss. At the most, they would only be responsible for four hours of programming out of a total of 2,920 prime time hours they air over a two-year period. It is likely that some stations already voluntarily exceed four hours of political programming per election.

This method for avoiding urban glut was also favored by the candidates. Of all the mechanisms for alleviating urban glut in the Center's survey, permitting broadcasters to allocate responsibility for different races among themselves received the highest support: 50.6 percent of candidates and 50.7 percent of incumbents supported this proposal.

This proposal also illustrates ways to overcome some of the other practical objections often raised to free media. Scheduling the presentations in half-hour blocks during the prime time access period avoids preempting only portions of scheduled programs. Simultaneity helps to ensure a wide audience and institutionalize a time when political broadcasts will always appear. For example, to prevent House and Senate races from competing with each other for the viewer's attention, and to regularize the appearances, the four Mondays before the election might be set aside for House races and the four Tuesdays before the election for the Senate race. Furthermore, forcing all stations to air free media at the same time reduces the ability of stations to all choose to feature the candidates from the same race.

The proposal outlined here limits free media requirements to general elections. This approach does sacrifice the effectiveness of free media in the minority of areas where primaries are critical, in order to make the concept workable overall. But it should be noted that the free media scheme recommended here is limited and experimental. After experience is gained with the new scheme in general elections, it could be extended to primary races if appropriate. The proposal could also be extended to gubernatorial races, as well as any other state and local races of particular interest.

In the meantime, broadcasters serving markets with a contested primary race should voluntarily set aside an amount of time comparable to the four half-hour programs recommended here, in order to present debates exempted from equal opportunities. The stations themselves can best judge whether there is sufficient interest in a primary race to justify airing a debate. Because debates are exempted from the equal opportunities rule, a broadcaster could air a debate between three front-running primary candidates without also presenting other, more obscure candidates in the same party's primary.

In summary, the free media proposal outlined above would provide an important first step in increasing the number of candidates' substantive appearances on the air. Its limited nature would give both broadcasters and candidates a chance to test free media's effectiveness. But by itself, it would not substantially reduce the cost of campaigns.

Succeeding chapters, therefore, examine a number of ways to reduce the cost of campaign ads, and to encourage stations voluntarily to provide additional time for candidate appearances. These are proposals worth considering, whether or not Congress enacts a free media requirement.

5.

Discounted Rates and Other Regulation of Political Advertisements

> *Politicians, being an occasional client of stations, were being sold the worst time for the highest prices... So what we decided to do in 1971 was to go for lowest unit rate, which simply put politicians on a parity with the best customers of a station, not the worst. And that worked for a while until stations figured it out — there are ways to cook the books.*
>
> *—Robert Squier*
> *Media Consultant*
> *Squier-Eskew Communications*

Although proponents often cite free media as an elixir that will both improve the quality of political debate and reduce campaign costs, these two goals may require different approaches. If the main goal is to improve the quality and tone of campaign debate, then proposals granting candidates a half-hour of free time most directly address these concerns. However, if any reform is to reduce campaign costs, it must either prohibit, or reduce the cost of, commercial-length advertisements that candidates would normally purchase.

A number of recent proposals seek either to reform the laws governing candidates' existing right to buy air time at the lowest unit rate, or grant candidates a new, additional discount. As discussed in Chapter Three, since the enactment of the 1971 Campaign Act, the law has sought to provide candidates a discount on the rates they must pay for TV and radio advertising. However, largely because industry practices have changed since 1971, the current law is not providing most candidates a significant discount.

One provision of H.R. 295, introduced in the 100th Congress by Rep. Anthony C. Beilenson (D-CA), would strengthen enforcement of the lowest unit rate law by changing its definition. Rep. Swift's H.R. 2464 would eliminate the lowest unit rate and replace it with a flat 30 percent discount on political advertising for all candidates who agree to certain spending limitations.

The proponents of discounting do not claim their proposals will necessarily improve public debate (although as discussed in Chapter Two, 30-second spots may inform some segments of the electorate). Their chief aim is to reduce campaign costs. But discounted advertising rates alone may not be enough to achieve cost reductions. A 50 percent discount on advertising, for example, could merely allow candidates to purchase up to twice as many ads.[1] Consequently, to guarantee true spending reductions, some argue that discounts to candidates must be made contingent upon candidates accepting some spending limitations. Swift's H.R. 2464, for example, takes this approach. It ties discounted advertising to limitations on aggregate spending. Other proposals would impose content restrictions on ads in a more direct effort to control the substance of political broadcasting. These issues, and the results of the Center's survey, are reviewed below.

1. The Adoption of Lowest Unit Rate

The legislative history of the lowest unit rate provisions illustrates the political and legal cross-currents likely to characterize proposals to reform the law today. It is also important to understand Congress' original intent in adopting the lowest unit rate requirement when assessing the law's current effectiveness, and proposals for changing it.

Lowest unit rate originated as a compromise measure, a proposal acceptable to broadcasters who wished to reduce the likelihood that Congress would require them to offer much deeper discounts for political advertising.

In 1969, the National Committee for an Effective Congress (NCEC), a liberal political action committee founded in 1948 by Eleanor Roosevelt, drafted legislation attempting to deal with the growing problem of the high cost of political campaigns, particularly advertising.

Russell D. Hemenway, NCEC's executive director since 1966, told the Center that he became alarmed by the cost of the 1968 elections, which he attributed to skyrocketing television rates: "I was incensed by the prices candidates were being charged by stations. I'm not only talking about the networks, but the thousands and thousands of small broadcasters across the country who were gouging candidates."

The NCEC bill was introduced in both houses of Congress on September 10, 1969. It guaranteed each legally qualified candidate for Congress an opportunity to buy substantially discounted television time on each station

---

[1] Of course, this assumes a perfectly elastic demand for advertisements, an unlikely occurrence. Any discounting of advertisements will likely yield *some* cost reductions.

which served at least one-third of a candidate's district. Broadcasters would make available spot commercial time at a 70 percent discount from their normal rates, and make program time available at an 80 percent discount.[2]

Former Senate Communications Subcommittee chief counsel Nicholas Zapple told the Center that the 38 Senate co-sponsors of the NCEC bill impressed him: "It created a pressurized environment . . . the bill was instrumental in getting us to hold hearings," hearings which led to consideration of the Political Broadcast Act of 1970.

The partisan concerns of the Democrats also played a role in spurring interest in the NCEC bill. In 1970, many Democratic Senators were facing tough reelection contests in which they knew their Republican opponents could outspend them on broadcasting.

The major opposition to the NCEC bill came from broadcasters and in particular the NAB. According to one account, however, the NAB played a low-key role in lobbying against the NCEC bill because "of its attitude, shared by others in and out of Congress, that there was no real chance of the bill's passage despite numerous cosponsors and public declarations to the contrary."[3]

Former Senator John Pastore (D-RI), then Chairman of the Senate Communications Subcommittee, opposed the NCEC's discounts, believing that they were excessive and would merely "allow the rich guy to buy more TV time, the poor guy to buy some."[4] Pastore's aide, Nicholas Zapple, told the Center that there were also concerns about the constitutionality of discount proposals: "Every time . . . the First Amendment would come up . . . the constitutional question always worried me."

As a result, Senator Pastore proposed the concept of the "lowest unit rate." Zapple felt that the lowest unit rate would avoid the constitutional difficulties: "If the broadcasters themselves were willing to make commercial time available at this rate, why not make it available to candidates," he told the Center.

---

[2] Senate candidates would be entitled to a minimum of 120 one-minute spots or their equivalent; House candidates would be permitted to buy 60 one-minute spots. Both House and Senate candidates would receive one thirty-minute program slot. The NCEC bill did not require that a certain percentage of the spots be offered in prime time.

[3] Robert L. Peabody, et. al. *To Enact A Law: Congress and Campaign Financing.* N.Y., Praeger Publishers, 1972, p. 65. The book details the development and passage of the 1970 Political Broadcast Act.

[4] *Ibid* at p. 91.

Moreover, some candidates were already receiving the lowest unit rate. CBS President Frank Stanton testified that his network voluntarily granted what it called an "end rate," virtually identical to lowest unit rate. In 1970 House testimony, ABC Vice President and General Counsel Everett H. Erlich estimated the lowest unit rate at "something on the order of 25 to 30 percent" and noted that this discount was "probably less than ABC is willing, voluntarily, to grant, incidentally."

As discussed in Chapter Three, the Political Broadcast Act of 1970, which also placed an overall cap on the amount candidates could spend on broadcast time and repealed the equal opportunities rule, was vetoed by President Nixon. When 1971 Campaign Act was enacted, it contained the same provisions on lowest unit rate as were in the 1970 bill.

All accounts indicate that lowest unit rate succeeded in reducing campaign costs during the first few elections. But since 1971 most television stations and some radio stations have abandoned the use of rate cards with set advertising rates, adopting in its place a system best described as an auction. Political consultants, campaign managers, and members of Congress all agree that in the decade and a half since it took effect, lowest unit rate has become eviscerated by changes in the way broadcasters sell advertising time. Understanding why lowest unit rate no longer provides meaningful discounts to candidates necessitates a look into the arcane world of media buying.

2. Impact of Current Industry Practices on Lowest Unit Rate

Today, as in 1971, broadcasters make available most advertising time on either a preemptible or a nonpreemptible basis.[5] Fixed, or nonpreemptible time, is the most expensive class of time, guaranteeing the advertiser a specific time slot that no other advertiser can bump. A less expensive class is preemptible time, spots which can be bumped by an advertiser willing to pay a higher rate, so long as the station gives the first advertiser some notice.

"Immediately preemptible" spots, typically priced about 50 percent below the fixed rate, may be preempted by a higher priced ad without any notice.

Preemptible Time. In 1971, once a station sold an ad on a preemptible basis, it was unlikely to resell the time to another advertiser except on a fixed basis. Today, by way of contrast, most television stations resell preemptible time to whichever potential advertiser is willing to pay the most for the preemptible time. The grid cards on the following pages, from two NBC

---

[5] Another category, run-of-station time, is the least expensive class of time. Because it allows the station to select the times the spots will appear, it is rarely used by candidates.

affiliates, one in a large market and one in a small market, illustrate the range of rates a station may offer advertisers.

With the aid of computers the station will continually replace purchases of lower-priced preemptible ads with advertisers willing to pay more for the time, all the way up to air time. Instead of relying on a rate card as they generally did in 1971 when the lowest unit rate requirement was enacted, television stations today thus essentially auction preemptible time to the highest bidder.

As Republican media buyer Bob Frank described the current system to the Center, "Broadcast buying is like a Middle East rug market."

Under the current system, it may be difficult to determine the lowest unit rate for a particular time. Though Congress intended the lowest unit rate to be the lowest rate a broadcaster charged any advertiser, stations today often interpret this to mean that a spot "must fit into its computer system at a rate that will not result in its being bumped by that day's higher-priced sales."[6] Though this is the lowest unit rate in the sense that it is the lowest charge that can get the advertiser on the air that day at that time, it does not give candidates the discount Congress envisioned in 1971.

Nonpreemptible Time. The lowest unit rate also requires stations to sell nonpreemptible time to candidates at the lowest rate at which this class of time is sold. Because candidates want assurance that a critical spot will air at the time they desire, they generally prefer nonpreemptible time despite its higher cost, and will generally buy such time to the extent the campaign's financial resources permit. Candidates, more than other advertisers, aim to move public opinion quickly, so they cannot afford to have their advertisements preempted.

It is too soon to know if these concerns will be eased by the FCC's announcement August 4, 1988 that a station must run before the election any candidate ad bumped from its original spot, if the station has a policy to "make good" in a similar manner a favored commercial advertiser's time-sensitive ads, such as one promoting a Memorial Day sale.

Media consultant Frank Greer told the Center: "I don't know of a campaign in their right mind that doesn't buy fixed time. You're crazy, in the pressure of a campaign, if you don't."

---

[6] Testimony of William Murphy, President of Media Management Services, before The Task Force on Elections, Committee on House Administration, July 21, 1983, p. 73.

Grid Card for WHAG, Hagerstown, MD
An NBC Affiliate

Rates for 30 second spots, Monday - Friday		F	I-1	I-2	I-3
AM					
6:00 - 6:30	Jimmy Swaggart	$25	20	15	10
6:30 - 7:00	NBC News Sunrise	$40	30	20	15
10:00 - 12:30	NBC AM Rotation (game shows)	$60	50	40	30
PM					
12:30 - 4:00	NBC PM rotation	$85	70	55	40
4:00 - 4:30	We Love the Dating Game	$90	75	60	45
4:30 - 5:00	The Newlywed Game	$110	90	75	60
5:00 - 6:00	Oprah Winfrey	$110	90	75	60
6:00 - 7:00	News 25 Alive	$200	165	125	90
7:00 - 7:30	Wheel of Fortune (Mon - Sat)	$200	165	125	90
7:30 - 8:00	Jeopardy (Mon-Sat)	$200	165	125	90

Prime Time (8:00 - 11:00 Monday - Saturday, 7:00 - 11:00 Sunday)

	Fixed: $600	I-1: $550	I-2: $500	I-3: $450
	I-4: $375	I-5: $275	I-6: $200	I-7: $150

Late Night		F	I-1	I-2	I-3
11:00 - 11:30	News 25 Alive Late Edition	$175	130	100	80
11:30 - 12:30	Tonight Show	$90	70	50	30
12:30 - 1:30	Late Night with David Letterman	$40	30	20	15

Notes
F - Fixed (non-preemptible) rate.

I - Immediately preemptible rate. I-1, I-2 and I-3 indicates that this station begins auctioning this time, all of which is preemptible without any notice, at three different prices.

N.B.: The grid card merely sets parameters for station's selling of time. The actual rates, in the event of an auction, will generally differ from these rates.

Source: Compiled by the center for Responsive Politics from data in *Spot Television Rates and Data, June 15, 1987.*

Grid Card for WDIV, Detroit, MI
An NBC Affiliate

Rates for 30 Second spots, Monday through Friday

	F	P1	P2	P3	P4	P5	P6	P7	P8
AM									
6:00 -7:00 NBC Sunrise/News 4 Today	$560	420	360	310	265	225	190	160	135
7:00 - 9:00 Today Show	$560	420	360	310	265	225	190	160	135
9:00 - 10:00 Donahue	$560	420	360	310	265	225	190	160	135
10:00 - noon Morning Rotation	$560	420	360	310	265	225	190	160	135
PM									
Noon - 1:00 12 O'Clock Live	$560	420	360	310	265	225	190	160	135
1:00 - 4:00 Afternoon Rotation	$560	420	360	310	265	225	190	160	135
4:00 - 5:00 Gimme A Break/Jeffersons	$875	700	600	530	460	400	345	300	250
5:00 - 6:00/6:00 -6:30 Monday - Sunday, News 4	$1150	925	800	700	600	530	460	400	350
7:00 - 7:30 Jeopardy	$3500	3000	2600	2300	2000	1725	1500	1300	1150
7:30 - 8:00, Wheel of Fortune	$3500	3000	2600	2300	2000	1725	1500	1300	1150

Continued on next page

Grid Card for WDIV - Detroit, MI
(continued)

PrimeTime

	F	P1	P2	P3	P4	P5	P6	P7	P8
8:00 - 11:00 Monday - Saturday; 7:00 - 11:00 Sunday	$8700	7300	6300	5500	4800	4200	3600	3100	2600
8:00 - 11:00 Monday - Sunday, Prime ROS	$4600	3700	3200	2800	2400	2100	1800	1550	1350
11:00 - 11:30 News 4	$3500	3000	2600	2300	2000	1725	1500	1300	1150
11:30 - 12:30 Tonight Show	$1250	1000	800	700	600	530	460	400	350
12:30 - 1:00 Barney Miller	$575	460	400	350	300	275	230	200	175
1:00 - 2:00 David Letterman	$375	300	275	230	200	175	155	135	120

Notes

F - Fixed Rate Time.
P1 - P8 Indicates eight different prices for immediately preemptible time, time which is preemptible at the discretion of the station without notice.
ROS- Run of Station, a rate generally lower than preemptible time that allows the station discretion over when the spots will air.
N.B.: The grid card merely sets parameters for station's selling of time. The actual rates, in the event of an auction, will generally differ from these rates.

Source: Compiled by the Center for Responsive Politics from data in *Spot Television Rates and Data*, June 15, 1987.

A different problem from that affecting preemptible time has rendered lowest unit rate largely meaningless for nonpreemptible time. In 1971, candidates could receive a discount on nonpreemptible time because many stations offered volume discounts to their most frequent advertisers. Few stations continue this practice today, and few commercial advertisers actually purchase nonpreemptible time at all. As a result, nonpreemptible time is usually a single rate for each particular time slot, without substantial volume discounts for favored customers. Because there is little variation in the rate, lowest unit rate barely helps candidates obtain nonpreemptible time more cheaply.

Another problem with lowest unit rate, especially as it applies to nonpreemptible time, is that some consultants believe that broadcasters, cognizant of the lowest unit rate requirement, "cook the books." Media consultants and media buyers have told the Center that stations typically cut off their special advertiser deals immediately before the period during which the lowest unit rate requirement applies. They raise their lowest price to a level they can comfortably tolerate for the 45 days before a primary and the 60 days before a general election. Even the FCC's Chief of Enforcement for Fairness and Political Programming, Milton O. Gross, observed to the Center that, "We have no way of knowing if they raise their rates. They don't publish them."

Seasonal variation of advertising rates explains at least part of the rise in prices. During the period from Labor Day to early November, the general election period, overall advertising demand is heavy because large businesses introduce new product lines and the holiday shopping season is approaching. Advertising rates are therefore generally higher in the fall. During this busy season, stations sometimes have to bump more profitable advertising to make way for political ads, thereby creating friction with more regular advertisers.

Although campaign managers and media consultants vigorously maintain that "book cooking" occurs, broadcasters deny the charges just as strenuously. One television sales manager with whom the Center spoke denied "jacking up all of our rates," but he admitted, "You *will* say to yourself, we have an election coming in the fall, and you'll look around to see if there are any skeletons in your closet, such as a low-priced spot in a hot time of day."

Finally, because lowest unit rate only applies during the 45 days before a primary and the 60 days before a general election, it provides no cost reductions for spots aired earlier in the campaign. While authors of the lowest unit rate hoped this restriction would shorten the period of active campaigning, some candidates have not been dissuaded from airing spots earlier. For example, North Dakota Senator Mark Andrews began airing ads for his November 1986 Senate race in October 1985.

The Center's Survey. Because these difficulties with lowest unit rate had previously only been detailed in an anecdotal manner, the Center included questions on lowest unit rate in its survey. First, the Center asked candidates whether they preferred "to purchase higher priced, nonpreemptible advertising time, or lower cost preemptible time." Of the candidates surveyed, 54.2 percent chose nonpreemptible time, 28.0 percent preferred preemptible time, and 17.8 percent chose both.

Incumbents, with larger campaign war chests which make possible more expensive media buys, were more likely to choose nonpreemptible time (62.0 percent nonpreemptible, 24.0 percent preemptible) than were challengers (48.0 percent nonpreemptible, 40.0 percent preemptible).

Those candidates who chose nonpreemptible time generally did so because they desired some sort of control over the placement of their ads. As one respondent put it, "In a political campaign you want as much control [as possible] over what is said, when it is said, and by whom." Another cited a desire to avoid being placed at the mercy of the "political ideology of the scheduler and/or management of the broadcaster." In some districts, candidates felt their spots had to be broadcast during particular hours (such as early morning in rural areas) in order to reach an audience with the desired demographics. Other campaigns chose nonpreemptible time so that they could effectively coordinate their spots with phone bank activity and other voter outreach programs.

Those candidates who chose preemptible time generally did so for budgetary reasons. One candidate noted, "We were on such a shoestring budget." Many in the survey who bought preemptible time only did so after being assured by consultants that their spots were unlikely to be bumped.

The Center's survey also revealed that most candidates, while more interested in nonpreemptible time than the less expensive preemptible time, did seek to buy time at the lowest unit rate. Of those polled, 63.4 percent sought time at the lowest unit rate, 17.9 percent said they had not, and 18.6 percent were unsure. Candidates in larger markets, who use less broadcast advertising, were particularly uncertain about the term "lowest unit rate." In particular, 31.3 percent of candidates in the six largest markets did not know whether they had sought time at the lowest unit rate.

Overall, most broadcast stations granted the request for time at what the station termed "the lowest unit rate" (73.0 percent of candidates who asked for it said they had received the discount, 7.0 percent said they had not, 17.4 percent sometimes received the lowest unit rate, and 2.6 percent were unsure). However, even some candidates who received the lowest unit rate complained it did not give them a meaningful discount: "A joke! . . . I think this rate was the 'lowest unit rate' but the rate I was offered was three times as high as the rate I could get as a businessman for my business."

The Center's open-ended questions also revealed candidate discontent over the way broadcasters interpret lowest unit rate. One respondent complained, "Stations need to sell time in a way that is consistent with federal policies. It varies from station to station." Others believed that the process of buying advertising time was too complex: "If you don't use a buyer or media placement company, broadcasters are not informative." Another commented, "People without media experience can have trouble."

3. Proposals to Change Lowest Unit Rate

Observers differ over how to adjust lowest unit rate to reflect current broadcast realities. One option is to retain the lowest unit rate without any changes, but improve its enforcement and clarify its meaning administratively. NCEC's Russell Hemenway, one of the law's original crafters, maintains that no additional legislation is necessary to implement the requirement effectively: "Lowest unit rate says, what is the cheapest possible rate? Surely someone can tell you that." Another father of the law, Nicholas Zapple, told the Center that his child is alive and kicking: "As difficult as it is to prove, there's still an obligation that the lowest unit rate be made available."

Another option is to make legislative changes in how lowest unit rate is defined. Henry Geller suggests that Congress require broadcasters to interpret it as, "the lowest rate you gave anyone for that time, on any basis, and you can't preempt it." Geller argues that if Congress would make that change, "all of a sudden lowest unit rate becomes very simple and very enforceable." This redefinition of lowest unit rate would provide candidates a further discount than they receive today by offering *nonpreemptible* time at the lowest rate the broadcaster charges for *preemptible* time for comparable periods.[7]

H.R. 295, a full public financing bill introduced by Rep. Beilenson, utilizes the Geller approach, requiring radio and television stations to offer candidates nonpreemptible time at the lowest preemptible rate offered for comparable time during the preceding 12 months. In addition to giving political candidates the lowest offered rate, this bill's reliance on the station's rates for an

---

[7] A review of the legislative history of lowest unit rate shows that Congress nearly provided candidates with nonpreemptible time at the lowest preemptible rate. The legislation passed the Senate Commerce Committee in 1970 containing only the restrictions that the lowest unit rate be governed by comparison to other rates charged for the same amount of time during the same time period. Indeed, the Committee report specifically stated that lowest unit rate "would provide that the highest rate a broadcast station could charge the candidates for fixed time for political campaign purposes would be the immediately preemptible rate." *Legislative History of the Federal Election Campaign Act of 1971,* The Federal Election Commission, September 1981, p. 28. However, when the bill reached the Senate floor, Sen. Ted Stevens (R-Alaska) introduced an amendment specifying that lowest unit rate only applied to the same "class" (meaning category) of time. The amendment was agreed to without a vote, entitling candidates to fixed rate time only at the lowest fixed rate sold for that period.

entire year would discourage broadcasters from changing the rates just before a campaign season begins.

Rep. Swift's bill, HR 2464, takes a third approach by replacing lowest unit rate with a flat percentage discount. Swift gives candidates a 30 percent discount from broadcasters' "normal and usual" rates, which would be determined by the FCC. Despite Swift's firm belief that lowest unit rate is outmoded, his bill in essence restores the original intent of the lowest unit rate since, as discussed earlier in this chapter, the value of the lowest unit rate discount was originally estimated at about 30 percent. Swift's discount represents a larger discount than many candidates are today receiving, especially on nonpreemptible time. In practice, however, the Swift bill would not eliminate all uncertainty over what rates candidates must be charged. The "normal and usual" rate might be as difficult to determine as lowest unit rate, but the FCC, rather than candidates and broadcasters, would grapple with its complexities.

Rep. Swift believes that the 30 percent discount his bill specifies is small enough that it would not overburden urban broadcasters. Most urban candidates today find television economically inefficient and prohibitively expensive; most would still refrain from buying television time, even with a 30 percent discount. Similarly, Swift argues that his bill would provide little benefit to the non-serious challengers who would not have funds to purchase television time even at a discount.

4. The Politics of Reforming Lowest Unit Rate

The Center's survey indicated that discounted advertising may attract significant support. The results of the survey are summarized in the chart on the following page. Overall, a plurality of respondents (46.2 percent to 38.5 percent) favored requiring broadcasters "to sell both nonpreemptible and preemptible time at a substantially discounted rate to candidates."

However, discounted advertising, like free media, proved less popular among incumbents. Only 27.0 percent of incumbents favored this proposal, while 48.6 percent were opposed. Discounted advertising was considerably more popular among challengers and open-seat candidates. While Democrats favored discounted advertising by a 54.3 percent to 30.9 percent margin, Republicans opposed the concept, 38.6 percent to 45.5 percent.

Senator McConnell has indicated in public statements that while Republicans could not accept public financing of campaigns, they are interested in crafting a bill which would contain new rules on lowest unit rate.

Views of Survey Respondents on Discounted Advertising Proposals

Question:

"Would your candidate favor providing free or discounted time to candidates on radio, television or cable in one or more of the following ways: Require broadcasters to sell both nonpreemptible and preemptible time at a substantially discounted rate to candidates?"

	Overall	
Yes	46.2%	
No	38.5%	
No Opinion	15.4%	

	Winners	Losers
Yes	27.9%	65.1%
No	51.2%	25.3%
No Opinion	20.9%	9.6%

	Democrats	Republicans
Yes	54.3%	38.6%
No	30.9%	45.5%
No Opinion	14.8%	15.9%

	House	Senate
Yes	45.5%	48.6%
No	41.0%	28.6%
No Opinion	13.4%	22.9%

	Incumbents	Challengers	Open Seat
Yes	27.0%	63.8%	53.8%
No	48.6%	29.0%	34.6%
No Opinion	24.3%	7.2%	11.5%

By Size of Markets — House Only (ADI Rankings)

	1-6	7-25	26-65	66 & up
Yes	58.1%	45.2%	17.9%	57.6%
No	32.3%	52.4%	50.0%	27.3%
No Opinion	9.7%	2.4%	32.1%	15.2%

n = 169

Source: Center for Responsive Politics

The NAB opposes lowest unit rate and considers it unconstitutional. As NAB President Edward Fritts told the Center, "If you provide a discount for television, why not give candidates a discount for all of their expenses: provide discounted air fares, discounted printing . . ." The NAB also views the current lowest unit rate as an unconstitutional infringement on the First Amendment freedoms guaranteed to all the press, including the broadcast press.[8]

On the other hand, Craig Smith, President of the Freedom of Expression Foundation, an organization which was formed to support the industry's First Amendment rights, told the Center, "I don't have much quarrel with lowest unit rate." It also appears that some individual stations may voluntarily be providing political discounts which go beyond the lowest unit rate required by law. One chain of television stations which the Center contacted makes a practice of issuing a "political rate card" that sets rates below the lowest unit rate. This has the significant effect of giving candidates a discount on fixed rate time, as well as on preemptible time.

Nevertheless, the debate early in 1988 over the general campaign finance reform bill in the 100th Congress, S. 2, suggests that reform of lowest unit rate law is one area of campaign finance reform where there may be an emerging bipartisan consensus. During negotiations over the fate of S. 2, a group of four Republicans led by Sen. Mitch McConnell and four Democratic Senators led by Sen. Boren, agreed on a proposal to define lowest unit rate as the lowest price charged any commercial advertiser for that time during the previous year. However, one aide to Boren told the Center that Boren's acceptance of this proposal was contingent upon the Republicans agreeing to use the new lowest unit rate as an incentive for overall spending limitations. The Republicans' unwillingness to agree to such a cap scuttled the package.

5. Expenditure Limits

Both free media and discounts on advertising would more effectively reduce campaign costs if the law required candidates to accept limits on media spending or overall campaign spending in exchange for such benefits. Congress in the past has actually enacted spending limits, limited just to expenditures on media. But for both practical and constitutional reasons the experiment was not a lasting one.

Historical Background. In 1970 Congress adopted a limit on broadcast spending in the Political Broadcast Act, but President Nixon vetoed it, due to pressure from Republican party leaders and strategists, who argued that the bill's broadcast spending restrictions would work to the advantage of incumbents,

---

[8] Testimony of Edward O. Fritts, President and CEO of NAB before the House Elections Subcommittee, Committee on House Administration, July 14, 1987.

and thus help freeze the Democrats' majority in Congress. The bill also worked against Nixon's party because Republicans had outspent Democrats on broadcasting in 1968 congressional races by a two-to-one margin. In his veto message, Nixon argued that the bill would leave spending on nonbroadcast media unrestricted: "The problem with campaign spending is not radio and television: the problem is spending. This bill plugs only one hole in a sieve." Nixon attacked the bill as an "incumbent's measure." The incumbent with "a natural avenue of public attention through the news media in the conduct of his office — would have an immeasurable advantage" over the little-known challenger struggling for name recognition. He also reasoned that candidates "would simply shift their advertising out of radio and television and into other media — magazines, newspapers, billboards, pamphlets, and direct mail." Finally, President Nixon argued that a fixed limit on spending would unfairly hurt urban candidates, for whom broadcast time was more expensive.

The 1971 Campaign Act resurrected and modified the broadcast spending limitations contained in the vetoed 1970 legislation. The law limited the amount that could be spent on all communications media, not just the broadcast media, to ten cents per eligible voter, or $50,000, whichever was greater. For subsequent elections, the Act's limitations would have risen in proportion to increases in the Consumer Price Index. To overcome President Nixon's objection that the 1970 Act discriminated against broadcast media, the term "communications media" included not only radio and television but also newspapers, magazines, and billboards. Candidates could use up to 60 percent of the limit, or six cents per voter, for broadcast advertising time.[9]

The limitations' effectiveness became the subject of much debate. Although broadcast spending in 1972 House and Senate races did decline from 1970, part of the decline may have resulted from the presidential campaigns which, as is normally the case in Presidential elections, siphoned off some funds that otherwise would have been used for congressional races. In addition, the availability for the first time of lowest unit rate helped cut campaign spending.

---

[9] In practice, these media ceilings meant that a House candidate could spend no more than $52,150 for all media, and $31,290 for radio and television. The radio and TV limits for Senate races ranged from $31,290 (in the smallest states) to $850,000 (in California). The limits also applied to the 1972 presidential elections, using the same formula: for 1972 the overall media limit was $14.3 million.

For whatever reasons, very few candidates in 1972 bumped up against the Act's limits on broadcast spending.[10]

The 1974 amendments to the Federal Election Campaign Act repealed the cap on media expenditures. Many members argued that a flat spending limit on media was too inflexible because TV advertising costs varied greatly from district to district. They favored instead a spending limit for *all* campaign costs to allow the candidate greater flexibility, and such a limit was passed. This in turn, of course, was struck down by the Supreme Court.

In its 1976 decision, *Buckley v. Valeo,* the Supreme Court, equating money with speech, struck down the aggregate spending limitations as an abridgment of First Amendment rights to freedom of speech.[11] Consequently, under current law, spending limits cannot be imposed unless candidates voluntarily agree to them, such as pursuant to the public financing scheme now made available to presidential candidates.

Current Proposals. Some see reform of the lowest unit rate laws as an opportunity to impose spending limits as well which comply with *Buckley v. Valeo,* but which avoid the need for a politically unpopular public financing scheme.

Congressman Swift, for example, favors discounts on ad rates not as an end in itself, but rather as a carrot that will induce candidates to accept overall spending limits. The Swift bill requires candidates to agree to a $200,000 aggregate spending limit for House primary and general elections ($400,000 for the entire election cycle) in exchange for certain benefits, including discounted broadcasting and discounted postage. The bill, S. 2 conditioned the availability of lowest unit rate on accepting spending and PAC limitations.

The proposal that candidates accept an aggregate spending limit *if* Congress passed a law mandating free time or discounted advertising won solid support in the Center's survey. Nearly 55 percent of those polled, including 48 percent of incumbents, supported this proposal. Nevertheless, a marked partisan split existed on this proposal: 75.6 percent of Democrats supported it, as opposed to only 36 percent of Republicans who supported it. Republicans

---

[10] In 1972 House general elections, only 18 of 754 candidates spent more than 90 percent of the Act's media limits. Because the spending cap was tied to increases in the Consumer Price Index and campaign costs rise at a faster rate than the CPI, more candidates would have reached the limits in 1974, had the law not been amended. *See* David W. Adamany and George E. Agree, *Political Money: A Strategy for Campaign Financing in America*, Baltimore, Johns Hopkins Press, 1975, p. 79.

[11] Buckley v. Valeo, 424 U.S. 1 (1976)

filibustered against S. 2 precisely because they believed its spending limitations would hinder a challenger's efforts to gain name recognition, and thus freeze in the Democratic majority.

6. Restrictions on Ad's Content

In addition to reducing the cost of political advertisements, members of Congress have expressed interest in improving the quality of ads. Several bills before Congress require the candidate to appear personally in a significant proportion of the ad. These reform efforts serve two distinct purposes. Some members of Congress seek to regulate the content of political programming in order to force candidates to address the issues and speak substantively about their candidacies, either in ads or in free media presentations. Others view content restrictions as a way of discouraging negative advertisements.

Such content restrictions raise serious First Amendment problems if they are imposed on all candidates. But by making content requirements voluntary—a condition the candidate must accept to be eligible for federal assistance—the bills avoid these constitutional difficulties. Thus, many of the current proposals for content restrictions are tied to discounted advertising or free media proposals.

The NAB has supported a bill, S. 979, by Sen Daniel Evans (R-WA) that would attach content restrictions to use of the lowest unit rate. In order to prevent negative attacks by candidates who only make fleeting appearances in their ads, Sen. Evans' bill would redefine the "use" of a broadcast station, which legally triggers the right of candidates to the lowest unit rate. Today a candidate must only make an "identifiable" appearance in an ad to qualify for a "use." The Evans bill, however, would redefine "use" to require a candidate to be identifiable in 100 percent of a spot, thus making lowest unit rate contingent on a candidate appearing throughout the ad. One proposed compromise version of S. 2 included a provision requiring that candidates appear in at least 50 percent of an ad in order to receive the lowest unit rate.

Similar restrictions are tied to some Free Media proposals. Rep. Stratton's H.R. 521 and H.R. 1817, as well as Sen. Pell's S. 593, specify that no less than 75 percent of the free media time must be taken up with the candidate's own remarks. All presentations under these bills also must promote the "rational discussion and debate of issues," but the bills do not offer a definition of "rational discussion," nor do they spell out sanctions against those who violate it.[12]

---

[12] Other bills, such as Senator Daniel Inouye's (D-Hawaii) "talking heads" proposal, S. 577, require that all paid political advertisements on television must consist of only the candidate speaking to the camera. The proposal is not tied, however, to receipt of any benefit such as lowest unit rate.

According to the American Enterprise Institute study of campaign laws described in Chapter Four, many other democracies already impose content restrictions on free time presentations. France, for example, requires candidates in free time broadcasts only to speak directly to the camera from the studio. In West Germany, free party advertisements must consist of a direct appeal by a party to the voters.

Content restrictions are aimed most directly at improving the quality of debate, rather than reducing the cost of campaigns. But they may also have some indirect effect on media costs. Curtis Gans of the Center for the Study of the American Electorate believes the "talking heads" proposal would reduce campaign costs by "severely reducing production costs attendant to political advertisements. . . . costs which by the hurried and frequently changing nature of the political enterprise can run from 20 to 50 percent of total media costs"[13] Most likely, the "talking heads" proposal would only eliminate production costs arising from shooting footage on location, but would leave untouched expenses such as the hiring of a crew and the costs of the studio and equipment.

Certain content restrictions may enjoy more political support than free media. Negative advertising disproportionately hurts incumbents. And as a problem that is visible and irksome to the public, its elimination is more likely to generate grass-roots support than the more abstract issue of cutting campaign costs. As mentioned above, the NAB supports tying some content provisions to lowest unit rate provisions.

The Center in its survey found that a plurality of respondents supported content restrictions. Those queried responded to the proposition that candidates accepting free or discounted time must also "accept certain content regulations, such as requiring a candidate to appear personally in at least 75 percent of the air time used." Survey results indicated 44.6 percent either supported or strongly supported this proposal, while 35.6 percent were either opposed or strongly opposed. Content regulation is generally regarded as favoring incumbents (since it discourages negative attacks on incumbents' records). But only 25 percent of incumbents supported this proposal, as opposed to 69 percent of challengers.

Another proposal to control the content of the ads is known as "free response time." It would require broadcasters to provide free time to any candidate who is opposed in a paid advertisement financed by an independent expenditure. The purpose of the proposal is to discourage such independent expenditures, which are seen as predominantly negative in nature. The bills were introduced in response to the activities of the National Conservative Political Action

---

[13] Curtis Gans, Testimony before the Senate Administration Committee, Sept. 29, 1983, p. 502.

Committee, which launched negative ad campaigns in the early 1980s. Thus, these proposals are not motivated by a desire to increase air time for candidates so much as to reduce negative ads by independent groups. During the mid-1980s "free response time" received more attention in Congress than free media.

The first major free response time proposal, introduced as a response to a spate of negative ads in 1984, was Sen. John Danforth's (R-MO) 1985 "Clean Campaign Act." The Danforth bill not only provided free response time for candidates opposed by independent expenditures, but also gave candidates free response time whenever an opponent attacked them in an ad in which the opponent did not personally appear. Danforth hoped to force candidates to be directly accountable for their negative statements, thereby discouraging them from making such statements.

The Danforth bill met strong opposition from the American Civil Liberties Union (ACLU). The ACLU's legislative counsel, Barry Lynn, termed it "an unconstitutional form of content-based discrimination."[14] The ACLU also believed the provision would largely benefit incumbents because challengers might not attack incumbents' records personally, at the risk of appearing heavy-handed.

Because the Danforth proposal elicited strong opposition, Sen.Boren's 1985 to 1986 campaign finance reform package incorporated only the provision granting free response time whenever an ad financed by an independent expenditure attacked the candidate. This became one of the centerpieces of Boren's PAC amendment, which the full Senate considered in August 1986.

A 1986 Congressional Research Service (CRS) analysis of the Boren provision maintained that it would discourage broadcasters from accepting advertisements by independent expenditure groups. Although the reasonable access rules require broadcasters to sell time to candidates, the same requirements do not apply to ads by independent committees. As a result, stations frequently reject these ads. As the CRS report concluded, "Faced with the certainty of triggering the provision of free response time for one or more opponents, broadcasters will likely be reluctant to accept any independent advertisements in the first place."

The CRS report also noted that because response time does not affect negative newspaper or direct mail ads, it would not completely shut off negative advertising. Furthermore, a group could sabotage the provision's intent by running an ad in which it ostensibly opposed a candidate it truly supported and

---

[14] *Campaign Practices Report*, Sept. 23, 1985, p. 5.

listed popular stands the candidate had taken. It would thus trigger response time for the candidate really favored by the group.[15]

The Boren free response time provision was defeated 58-42 by an amendment by Sen. Rudy Boschwitz (R-MN). It is not clear, however, that the Senate vote represented opposition just to free response time. The Boschwitz amendment also prohibited PAC contributions to political parties, and required political parties to disclose the receipt of "soft money" (money which is unregulated by the federal campaign laws, and which parties accept for non-federal purposes at the state and local level).

According to an aide to Sen. Boren, Boren interpreted the vote as the will of the Senate on free response time. Consequently, when he and Sen. Byrd reintroduced most of his PAC proposals as S. 2 in the 100th Congress, they dropped the free response time provisions. In the 100th Congress, the only free response time provision was introduced in the House by the late Rep. James Howard (D-NJ) as part of his bill regulating PACs (H.R. 166). Like the 1986 Boren incarnation of the proposal, it would grant free response time whenever an independent expenditure ad opposes a candidate.

7. Ban on Political Ads

Some critics who believe 30-second ads to be pernicious want to forbid candidates from purchasing any spot advertisements in exchange for providing candidates substantial blocks of free time. This approach would ensure that free media both reduced campaign costs and improved the political dialogue appearing in the media during a campaign. As discussed in Chapter Four, this system works effectively in many other democracies, including Great Britain.

Rep. Jacobs' free media bill, for example, grants candidates 90 minutes of television time in blocks of at least five minutes apiece (as well as radio time and newspaper space) if they agree not to accept any PAC contributions, and to place no additional media advertisements. This means a candidate could make a maximum of 18 five-minute appearances on TV during the campaign. It is unlikely that candidates would forgo the possibility of hundreds of shorter radio, TV, and newspaper ads for no more than 18 TV appearances.

Any proposal to ban political spots would constitute an "incumbent protection act" unless the free time offered were substantial enough to provide challengers a reasonable opportunity for exposure. As we discussed in Chapter Two, challengers commonly face a disadvantage in name recognition that only

---

[15] Congressional Research Service, *Campaign Finance Proposals to Limit PACs and to Grant Free Broadcast Time*, Appendix to Hearings on S.1806 before the Committee on Rules and Administration, 99th Cong. 2nd Sess., p. 344 (1986).

broadcast advertising can close. On the other hand, if legislation simply barred spot ads, rather than allowing candidates the option of forgoing such spots in exchange for free or discounted time, serious constitutional problems would also arise.

In the Center's survey, 38.4 percent of respondents either supported or strongly supported conditioning free time on candidates agreeing not to spend additional funds on air time; 51.2 percent opposed or strongly opposed it. As with content restrictions, incumbents were reluctant to change the status quo even though an advertising ban may be construed as a pro-incumbent proposal. Only 30 percent of the incumbents supported this proposal. A wide partisan split also existed. Among Democrats, 50.0 percent supported an advertising ban, while among Republicans, only 27.9 percent supported it.

8. Recommendations

The Center makes the following recommendations concerning discounted advertising rates and other regulation of campaign ads:

- Candidates should be entitled to preemptible time at the lowest preemptible rate provided any advertiser for that period over the previous year (excluding summer months). Such ads should not be preemptible except by an advertiser paying a nonpreemptible rate.

- For nonpreemptible time, candidates should receive a 30 percent discount from the station's average rate for that time during the previous year (excluding summer months).

- Congress should make a candidate's right to lowest unit rate contingent upon the candidate participating significantly in at least the audio portion of the ad.

Lowest Unit Rate. Free Media proposals may promote more substantive candidate appearances, but will probably not reduce campaign costs significantly. Therefore, the issue of cost needs to be addressed directly by revising the laws governing the advertising rates stations may charge candidates. Congress should clarify and strengthen the laws on lowest unit rate so that their impact is closer to what Congress intended in 1971.

The Center's survey confirmed that the law often proves ineffectual because 1) there is considerable confusion over how to apply the current law to the auction system that many stations use to sell preemptible time and 2) the rates for nonpreemptible time, which candidates are more likely to use, are now less subject to discounting or variation among commercial advertisers, thereby negating the usefulness of the lowest unit rate concept.

To realign lowest unit rate with current industry practices, candidates should be entitled to treatment as "preferred preemptible advertisers." Candidates buying preemptible time would receive the lowest preemptible rate, and could not be bumped by any other preemptible buy. Only an advertiser buying fixed rate time could bump a political advertiser. Since few commercial advertisers buy fixed time, candidates would, in practice, face little danger of preemption if they bought preemptible time under this system. While some have suggested that candidates should actually be entitled to nonpreemptible time at the lowest preemptible rate, this would violate the principle adopted in the 1971 Campaign Act that candidates' rates should be based on the rates paid by other advertisers for the same type of service.

Nonpreemptible time should be sold to political candidates at a flat 30 percent discount from the average rate charged for that time period over the past year. This would compensate for the elimination of volume discounting since 1971, and provide candidates with roughly the same discount for nonpreemptible time that lowest unit rate was originally intended to achieve.

Candidates should receive the lowest rate for preemptible time that a broadcast station granted any advertiser in the period between the previous September 15 and June 15 of the election year. Restricting the base period to these dates avoids having the rates skewed unrealistically by the lower rates charged during the summer months, when audience levels (and therefore advertising rates) are at their lowest. The average rate used as the basis for the 30 percent discount on nonpreemptible time would be calculated over the same period.

Ending the base period on June 15 would also give stations time to calculate their rates in advance of the general election period, permitting candidates to obtain adequate notice of the rates. Because the rates charged candidates for a particular time period would not change over the election period, candidates could plan their media budget with greater certainty. The base period for primaries occurring in the summer months (June 15-September 15) would be the rates charged by the station the previous summer. For other primary elections, the period used for determining the lowest unit rate would be the nine preceding non-summer months.[16]

Under this approach, at any particular time, on any given station, all candidates would then be entitled to a single preemptible or nonpreemptible rate

---

[16] As an example, for a May 15 primary, the lowest unit rate period would begin April 1, stations would have to publish their rates by March 1, and the lowest unit rate would be calculated based on rates during the nine preceding non-summer months, March 1 to June 15 of the previous year and September 15 to March 1 of the election year.

based on the station's rates for the previous year. Because the rates would be based on the actual experience of stations over an extended period, there is less likelihood of disagreement or confusion over the proper rate to be charged candidates.

In themselves, these changes may not reduce the overall amount campaigns spend on advertising, for lower rates could just permit candidates to stretch their dollars further. However, discounted advertising rates do reduce the amount of money candidates must raise to achieve a threshold level of media exposure. It is possible some candidates will simply buy more time if the costs are lower, but others might feel less pressure to raise campaign funds for last minute media blitzes, or may decide to reserve more funds for grass-roots campaign activities.

Conditioning Lowest Unit Rates on Candidate's Participation. As part of reform of the lowest unit rate law, Congress should condition receipt of lowest unit rate on the candidate's voice being heard and identified for some significant portion of the ad. A candidate should not receive a discount on advertising merely a picture of the candidate appears at the end of the advertisement, as is currently the case.

One survey respondent expressed support for so redefining "use" as it relates to lowest unit rate: "It's silly to get a cheaper rate if a candidate merely puts a tag line on at the end of a commercial." Significantly, this type of change has the support of both the NAB and the respondents to the Center's survey. Redefining "use" to require candidates to speak in the advertisements would require candidates to be more closely identified and involved with the advertisements they employ, and give the public some chance to hear the candidate.

Other Spending or Content Restrictions. The Center believes that free response time would have a detrimental effect and should not be adopted. Granting free response time whenever an ad paid for by an independent group attacks a candidate may be difficult to administer (particularly in determining when an ad opposes a candidate). But perhaps more significantly, it is likely to have a chilling effect on free speech, since broadcasters may refuse to air independent expenditure advertisements in order to avoid having to offer free ads in response.

Proposals which would ban political advertisements, either outright (which would raise First Amendment questions) or in exchange for a significant amount of free media time, would only make sense in conjunction with a comprehensive free media proposal, one which provided a greater quantity of time than the free media proposal outlined in Chapter Four. Unless such comprehensive free media schemes are adopted, it would be premature to ban all paid political advertisements.

Arguments for and against an overall spending cap extend beyond the scope of this monograph, and go to the heart of the current debate over this country's campaign finance laws generally. They raise significant partisan political issues which make any change of this nature very difficult. Nevertheless, if at some future date Congress wished to impose a cap on overall campaign spending it could condition use of discounted advertising rates on the candidate agreeing to comply with overall expenditure limits. Such a scheme avoids using "taxpayer dollars" to finance campaigns, and makes it constitutionally possible to place limits on campaign expenditures.

A revitalized law on lowest unit rate could be sufficiently attractive to candidates that they might be willing to accept conditions, such as an cap on expenditures, in exchange for the discount. As discussed above, the Center's survey disclosed a relatively high level of support for such an approach among candidates.

6.

Cable, Radio, and Public Broadcasting

> *With national cable penetration now past 50 percent of U.S. homes and the cost of political advertising on broadcast television continuing to escalate, the cable networks offer an audience that is better educated, more affluent, older than the voting age population as a whole, and more likely to vote.*
>
> *— Brian Conboy*
> *Vice President, Government*
> *Affairs, Time, Inc.*

Examination of the use of media by candidates often focuses exclusively on commercial television, the most glamorous and potent of the electronic media. Indeed, much of the current political broadcasting legislation — such as the Pell bill — aims its sights only at commercial television. But in many congressional campaigns, particularly in urban areas, the most important form of electronic media is not television but radio. Cable television, too, is beginning to open up new opportunities for politicians. And if public television manages to secure a new funding source, it could become an even more important outlet for political broadcasting. This chapter examines how different programming restraints and legal and financial considerations affect the role cable, radio, and public broadcasting plays in informing the voter.

1. Cable

For about two decades, cable television has tantalized the television industry with its enormous potential as a vehicle for candidates. Because cable franchises are awarded for a specific county or municipality, candidates can target specific geographic areas and specific groups of voters. The best example of the use of such "narrowcasting" using cable is Representative Barney Frank (D-MA.), whose successful election strategy in a new congressional district included airing commercials featuring local Portuguese businessmen on a cable channel serving Fall River's sizable Portuguese community. Candidates may also find cable advantageous because time is available outside of the strict 30- and

60-second constraints of commercial advertising. Even in the absence of any free media laws, cable TV offers a candidate today a variety of ways to obtain access to viewers at little or no cost.

Cable Programming Available to Candidates. Though the original cable systems, built in the 1950s and 1960s, generally had a capacity of 12 channels, most of which were broadcast channels from nearby towns and cities, some recently franchised state-of-the-art systems have the ability to transmit over 75 channels. This gives political candidates new opportunities for exposure.

Cable operators use some of the channels to retransmit the signals of the local UHF and VHF stations.[1] On these local channels, cable television is merely enhanced reception broadcast television; political broadcasting on these channels would be governed by the policies of the broadcast station that originated the program. Cable operators use other channels for programming which they or other members of the community originate specifically for cable. Cable's greatest potential for political broadcasting exists on these local access and local origination channels.

Congress, in the Cable Communications Policy Act, allowed local franchising authorities to designate three types of local access or "PEG" channels: 1) public access, produced by members of the community; 2) educational access, produced by local high schools and colleges; and 3) government access, reserved for coverage of local governmental bodies such as local city council or school board meetings.[2]

Almost all franchise agreements provide for these so-called PEG channels, creating what amounts to an electronic soapbox. "PEG" access channels are noncommercial, and make free production time and channel space available to groups or individuals. On all three types of channels, the cable

---

[1] The FCC initially required cable operators to transmit all local broadcasting stations, but these so-called "must-carry" rules have been struck down by the courts. See, e.g., Century Communications v. FCC 835 F. 2d 292 (D.C. Cir. 1987), 837 F.2d 517 (D.C. Cir. 1988). *See also* Quincy Cable TV, Inc. v. FCC, 768 F.2d 1434 (D.C. Cir. 1985), *cert. denied sub nom.* National Association of Broadcasting v. Quincy Cable TV, Inc., 476 U.S. 1169 (1986). Some cable operators (but not the National Cable Television Association) strongly oppose the "must-carry" rules because they limit their ability to carry more profitable cable services.

[2] The Cable Communications Policy Act of 1984 merely allows franchising bodies to establish such PEG requirements. Pub. L. No. 98-549, §2, 47 U.S.C. 531. Previously, the FCC in the Cable Television Report and Order, 36 FCC 2d 143 (1972), had administratively *required* systems with more than 3,500 subscribers to establish access channels.

operator merely makes available the facilities and channel space for the transmission, and has no say over the content. A fourth type of channel, leased access, allows commercial interests to lease space for programming. As members of the public, candidates could obtain free time on one or more of these local access channels if they desired.

Another option on most cable systems is "local origination channels," community-oriented programming that *is* produced by the cable operator. Cable operators generally program these channels with local sporting events, community billboards, high school drama productions, and other such programming. These channels are typically more commercial than access programming, and candidates can purchase time for ads during local origination programming. Because cable operators rarely fill their origination channels 24 hours a day, they could offer political candidates a great deal of time during election seasons either for individual presentations or for debates.

While local origination and local access channels offer plenty of time, they cannot offer candidates much of an audience. More than other cable channels, this locally produced programming draws a very small audience.

Finally, House and Senate candidates can currently purchase local advertisements on feeds from national cable services such as MTV, Cable News Network (CNN), etc. These national services allow local cable franchises various times called "local availabilities" or "avails" during which the local cable company can run advertising. As the national cable services are the most heavily watched part of cable, local avails provide an opportunity for candidates to purchase commercial time likely to reach an adequate audience.[3]

Current Use of Cable by Candidates. Even though cable has reached its long predicted levels of national penetration — just over half of American homes with TV sets now have cable television — politicians, in fact, still use cable only sparingly.

According to media buyer John Power, group Vice President of Vitt Media International in New York, candidates do not generally take advantage of the possibilities cable offers because political consultants are generally not well versed in cable, and are not yet confident that cable delivers a large enough audience. Power said in an interview with the Center that ratings for most

---

[3] Cable systems also offer pay channels, which are available to cable subscribers for an additional fee beyond the basic rate (typically $10-$12 each). Many of these pay channels, such as Home Box Office, offer unedited movies delivered by satellite 24 hours a day. Because the pay movie channels run unedited films without commercial interruption, there is no room for candidate spots, or other forms of political broadcasting.

individual cable channels are so low that candidates feel they cannot achieve much by advertising on cable. One of the respondents to the Center's survey noted that debates held on cable also do not help candidates gain exposure: "There is very little interest among uncommitted voters in cable TV programs of this nature."

The Center's survey confirmed that cable remains a minor factor in most House and Senate campaigns. In 1986, 83.1 percent of candidates in the Center's survey spent less than $10,000 on cable television. Only 3.1 percent of candidates spent $100,000 or more, and all of these were Senate candidates. Not one candidate surveyed said cable was the media form on which the campaign spent the most money.

Only 7.1 percent of general election debate offers were made solely by cable. On the other hand, cable was an important outlet for debates in the six largest media markets, where cable could offer an audience more closely segmented geographically by congressional district than commercial television can achieve. Survey results indicated 21.7 percent of the debates aired in these markets appeared on cable TV. The chart on the following page compares the use of different media for debates during the 1986 general election.

Cable and the Political Broadcasting Rules. Despite the great potential of cable as a forum for political candidates, there is considerable uncertainty about the extent to which political broadcasting rules apply to it. Changes which Congress made to the Communications Act in the 1971 Campaign Act had the effect of applying the equal opportunities and lowest unit rate rules to some cable programming. These changes define "broadcasting station" for purposes of Section 315 of the Communications Act to include the operator of any "community antenna television system" (the common term for cable television at the time).[4] The statutory language confirmed the FCC's prior application of the equal opportunities rules to cable.

Current FCC regulations apply these rules only to "origination cablecasting," which the regulations define as programming "subject to the exclusive control of the cable operator."[5] Spot advertising time which candidates buy during the local availabilities on national cable services such as CNN is, therefore, presumably subject to the equal opportunities and lowest unit rate rules. But a programming service such as CNN also includes national advertising and programs that originate with CNN rather than a local operator. Since current FCC regulations only apply the political broadcasting rules to programming "subject to the exclusive control of the cable operator," it is

---

[4] 47 U.S.C. 315(c). See Pub. L. No. 92-225, §104(c).
[5] 47 C.F.R. §76.5(r).

Debates Offered to House and Senate Candidates by Media Type

Overall

Type of Media	Percentage
CommercialTV	25.2%
Public TV	18.1%
Cable TV	7.1%
TV combination	14.2%
Commercial Radio	10.2%
Public Radio	3.1%
TV/ Radio combination	22.0%

By Chamber

	House	Senate
Commercial TV	24.8%	26.9%
Public TV	16.8%	23.1%
Cable TV	7.9%	3.8%
TV combination	11.9%	23.1%
Commercial Radio	12.9%	0.0%
Public Radio	3.0%	3.8%
TV/Radio combination	22.8%	19.2%

By ADI Market (House races only)

	1-6	7-25	26-65	66 & up
Commercial TV	34.8%	15.2%	29.4%	25.0%
Public TV	0.0%	27.3%	11.8%	21.4%
Cable TV	21.7%	0.0%	11.8%	3.6%
TV combination	4.3%	12.1%	23.5%	10.7%
Commercial Radio	17.4%	15.2%	5.9%	10.7%
Public Radio	4.3%	3.0%	0.0%	3.6%
TV/Radio Combination	17.4%	27.3%	17.6%	25.0%

n=127

Source: Center for Responsive Politics

unclear whether national programming, including advertisements, is subject to the equal opportunities and lowest unit rate rules as well.

Since most of cable television's popular programming comes from national cable services, exempting them from political broadcasting rules substantially reduces the rules' effectiveness, particularly for presidential races, where advertising may be bought nationally. Yet it would seem to be neither practical nor fair to make the local cable operator, who may not have any real control over the programming decisions of the national service, responsible for the political advertisements or programming of the national service. Similar confusion exists over whether the equal opportunities and lowest unit rate rules apply to programming on public access channels, which is not under the local cable operator's control.

The applicability of reasonable access is also in doubt. As discussed in Chapter Three, the reasonable access rules require licensees to make available air time for federal candidates who wish to purchase the time. After the 1971 changes, the FCC concluded in its primer on political broadcasting that the reasonable access rules also applied to cable TV. However, the FCC has subsequently questioned the applicability of reasonable access to cable, and no FCC regulations currently apply these rules to cable.[6]

A 1981 FCC report to Congress noted that the reasonable access rules might apply to cable on the grounds that the section in the 1971 legislation defining "broadcasting station" to include cable also applied to the changes adding the reasonable access rule. Subsequent amendments in 1974 to the Federal Election Campaign Act have reduced the force of that argument, however. The 1981 FCC report concluded, "it now appears that without further clarifying legislation or commission rulemaking that these rules [on reasonable access] could only be enforced against cable television systems operators with great difficulty, if at all."[7]

Since the statute's specific sanction for violation of the reasonable access rules — loss of license — cannot apply to cable operators who are not

---

[6] See Henry Geller and Donna Lampert, *Cable, Content Regulation and the First Amendment,* 32 Cath. U.L. Rev. 603, 606 (1983).

[7] Cable Television and the Political Broadcasting Laws: The 1980 Election Experience and Proposals for Change, Report to Senator Goldwater. Cable Television Bureau, Federal Communications Commission, January, 1981. p.24.

licensed by the FCC, it is unclear what sanctions would apply to a cable operator who violates the rules.[8]

In addition to these statutory questions, the constitutionality of subjecting cable operators to the existing laws remains unsettled. After over twenty years of government regulation of the industry, the judicial system has still not resolved which First Amendment principles apply to cable. Since the local cable operator does not broadcast signals, the number of cable stations is not restricted by any scarcity of broadcast frequencies. Some cable operators also argue that in the absence of such scarcity, the imposition of free media requirements would be an unconstitutional taking of property without due compensation. The United States Court of Appeals for the Eighth Circuit and for the District of Columbia have both ruled that cable television should be treated like the print media.[9]

On the other hand, another Court of Appeals held in *Community Communications Co., Inc. v. City of Boulder*,[10] that "government must have some authority . . . to see to it that optimum use is made of the cable medium in the public interest." In a recent Supreme Court case, Justice Blackmun commented that in assessing First Amendment claims concerning cable access, the court must determine whether the characteristics of cable television make it sufficiently analogous to another medium to warrant application of an already existing standard, or whether those characteristics require new analysis.[11]

None of the political broadcasting reform bills in the 100th Congress contained provisions that apply specifically to cable TV. Despite cable's growth

---

[8] Arguably, the FCC could invoke its general powers under Section 312(b) to order any person who violates the provisions of the Communications Act to "cease and desist".

[9] Both courts reiterated one of the key elements of Miami Herald Publishing Co. v. Tornillo: economic scarcity alone does not justify government regulation of speech. The court in Home Box Office, Inc. v. FCC, 567 F.2d 9, 46 (D.C. Cir. 1977) held that "there is nothing in the record before us to suggest a constitutional distinction between CATV and newspapers on this point." Similarly, in Midwest Video Corp. v. FCC, 571 F.2d 1025, 1043 (8th Cir. 1978), the court ruled that a cable system, unlike broadcasting, does not utilize a "limited and valuable part of the public domain." Consequently, the Court reasoned it should be treated like a private enterprise, with full First Amendment rights. The Supreme Court, in affirming the lower court's decision, did not touch upon the constitutional questions raised. Federal Communications Commission v. Midwest Video Corporation, 440 U.S. 689 (1979).

[10] 660 F.2d 1370, 1379 (10th Cir. 1981).

[11] City of Los Angeles and Dept. of Water and Power v. Preferred Communications, Inc., 476 US 488, 496 (1986).

and potential as a political tool, no statutory proposal has yet defined the legal requirements that should apply to political broadcasting on cable.

2. Radio

Radio has assumed a major role in House and Senate elections because it is a relatively cost-effective medium for political messages. Each radio ad costs much less than a comparable TV ad to produce. Yet, these savings are somewhat deceptive. The cost per rating point of air time (cost based on number of people reached) is about equal for radio and TV according to media consultant Ed Blakely.

Though radio and television both use scarce-spectrum space and are thus equally subject to government regulation, the two media face much different practical concerns. For example, commercial television stations seek to appeal to the entire viewing public, and therefore feature a broad mix of programming which is similar from station to station. Radio stations, on the other hand, differ greatly from one another. Most radio stations today choose one format (e.g., Top 40, classical, news, etc.), develop a distinct personality, and seek to attract listeners with specific tastes.

Perhaps radio's largest comparative advantage lies in the ability it gives candidates to target ads at specific groups of voters. A candidate seeking to reach the young voter could prepare an ad specially for use, for example, on the local "urban contemporary" radio station. Candidates seeking to reach politically-active, information-hungry voters with perhaps a different kind of ad are more likely to advertise on an all-news radio station.

These differences among radio stations caused broadcasters to suggest to the FCC in 1978 a degree of flexibility in applying the reasonable access doctrine to radio: "different sets of standards would apply to stations depending upon their formats — an "all news" station being required to provide more access to federal candidates than "beautiful music" stations."[12]

The chart on the following pages suggests that radio is an important, but not indispensable, instrument in House and Senate campaigns. It finished third, behind commercial television and direct mail, as the medium on which candidates spent the most money: 17.8 percent of those surveyed said their campaign spent the most money on radio, 20.3 percent in the House and 8.3 percent in the Senate. Only one House candidate in the Center's sample spent more than $100,000 on radio, and 92 percent of House candidates spent less than $50,000. Even in the Senate, only one candidate in the sample spent more than $250,000.

---

[12] 68 FCC 2nd. 1079, 1084 (1978). The broadcasters' request was not granted.

As is evident from the previous chart in this chapter on debates offered to House and Senate candidates by media type, radio took a back seat to television in the coverage of House and Senate debates. Only 10.2 percent of debates in the Center's survey were offered by commercial radio stations, and only 3.1 percent by public radio stations (although another 22.0 percent of debates were offered by some combination of radio and television stations). One possible explanation for radio's disappointing showing is that candidates want assurance of a larger audience and want to be seen by the public, not just heard.

3. Public Broadcasting

The Center's survey found that public television stations are already disproportionately active in airing House and Senate candidate debates. Even though each market has many fewer public television stations than commercial stations, nearly as many debates were offered by public television stations as by commercial stations. Public television stations offered 18.1 percent of debates against 25.2 percent by all commercial TV stations. These numbers may somewhat understate public broadcasting's participation because 14.2 percent of debates were offered by some combination of commercial, cable, and public television stations, and another 22.0 percent of debates were to be broadcast on some combination of television and radio stations, likely including public television stations. Of course, because public TV has no commercials, these stations carry no paid spots by candidates.

On the other hand, the low number of debates offered by public radio stations was particularly surprising given their generally more educated, politically active audience. However, many public radio stations are small and financially strapped. They may not have the news staffs or remote equipment necessary to stage and broadcast political debates. According to estimates provided to the Center by National Public Radio, only about 10 percent of member stations have the staff to produce news segments of their own.

Congress currently funds the Corporation for Public Broadcasting (CPB) so they may provide money to public radio and television stations for programming in the public interest. Currently, CPB does give "community service grants" to each public television station for public affairs programming, but does not specify how the grants should be spent. Some commercial broadcasters argue that since the government already funds public broadcasting, public broadcasters should assume any new political broadcasting obligations with the help of increased funding from CPB.

Mandating a greater role for public broadcasting raises a number of objections from public broadcasters who argue it could send the wrong signal to broadcasters, and create the wrong precedent. Congress would be implying that

Level of Spending by Candidates on Different Media

"During the 1986 campaign, on which type of communication did your campaign spend the most money?"

Overall

Commercial TV	50.6%
Radio	17.8%
Newspapers	7.5%
Direct Mail	23.0%
Other	1.1%

By Chamber

	House	Senate
Commercial TV	40.6%	88.9%
Radio	20.3%	8.3%
Newspapers	9.4%	0.0%
Direct Mail	28.3%	2.8%
Other	1.4%	0.0%

By Winner/Loser

	Winners	Losers
Commercial TV	52.2%	48.8%
Radio	17.4%	18.3%
Newspapers	5.4%	9.8%
Direct Mail	25.0%	20.7%
Other	0.0%	2.4%

By Party

	Democrats	Republicans
Commercial TV	54.1%	47.2%
Radio	22.4%	13.5%
Newspapers	4.7%	10.1%
Direct Mail	18.8%	27.0%
Other	0.0%	2.2%

Continued on next page

Level of Spending by Candidates *(continued)*

By Level of Competition

	Noncompetitive Races	Competitive Races
Commercial TV	37.4%	87.2%
Cable	0.0%	0.0%
Radio	16.8%	5.1%
Newspapers	10.3%	0.0%
Direct Mail	33.6%	7.7%
Other	1.9%	0.0%

By Incumbents/Challengers

	Incumbents	Challengers	Open Seats
Commercial TV	47.4%	46.4%	70.4%
Radio	17.9%	17.4%	18.5%
Newspapers	5.1%	11.6%	3.7%
Direct Mail	29.5%	21.7%	7.4%
Other	0.0%	2.9%	0.0%

By ADI Markets *(House respondents only)*

	1-6	7-25	26-65	66 & up
Commercial TV	12.5%	44.4%	57.1%	48.5%
Radio	18.8%	20.0%	17.9%	24.2%
Newspapers	15.6%	8.9%	3.6%	9.1%
Direct Mail	53.1%	22.2%	21.4%	18.2%
Other	0.0%	4.4%	0.0%	0.0%

n = 174

Notes

Competitive races — Races where candidate received between 40 and 60 percent of the vote.
Noncompetitive races — Races where candidate received less than 40 percent or over 60 percent of the vote.

Source: Center for Responsive Politics

although commercial broadcasters are public trustees, public broadcasting stations could relieve the commercial broadcasters of responsibility for political broadcasting. Ward Chamberlin, of public television station WETA-TV, told the Center that if public television shouldered the responsibility for free media, commercial broadcasters would no longer take on the responsibility on their own: "They would say, it's already taken care of . . . That's what's happened in other areas — opera, dance, drama — which commercial television doesn't do any more."

Shunting candidates to public broadcasting would also not satisfy candidates' need to reach a wide audience. Some candidates in the Center's survey complained that, as with cable TV, they were not confident that public television could reach voters effectively. For example, one challenger complained about a debate held on public TV, saying "It didn't help much — the public TV station only had a viewership of 1 percent."

Specifying that additional CPB funding must be used for political broadcasting would also raise concerns about government intervention in the station's programming decisions.

4. Recommendations

Because of the different economics of cable, radio and public broadcasting, compared to commercial TV, and the greater diversity of programming they can provide, these forms of electronic media have great potential as a way to inform the voter about the candidates. In applying political broadcasting rules to these media, the Center makes the following recommendations:

- Congress should clarify by statute that the laws governing political broadcasting, including the reasonable access rules, apply both to local cable operators and to national cable services.

- The particular free media scheme described in Chapter Four should be modified for radio. The FCC should develop guidelines which apply the proposal's principles to those radio stations that already carry a significant amount of news or public affairs programming as part of their regular format.

- Changes in the lowest unit rate rule should apply to cable and radio, as well as television.

- Associations serving cable owners or public broadcasting stations should work with the operators of such facilities to encourage more debates and other innovative election programming.

Cable. Cable may play an increasingly important role in campaigns. So long as it is felt desirable to regulate political broadcasting on radio and TV in order to promote the effective working of the democratic system, cable should be regulated for the same reason. Therefore, Congress should clarify by statute that reasonable access, just like the equal opportunities and lowest unit rate requirements, applies to cable. Since the cable operator does not operate pursuant to a license which may be lost in case of violations of the law, the legislation should provide for a civil fine against cable companies which violate these laws.

Congress should also specify that these requirements apply not only to the local cable operator, but also to cable's national programming services such as the USA Network or CNN.[13] All changes in the lowest unit rate rule suggested in Chapter Five should also apply to cable at both the local and the national level. On the other hand, it may not be appropriate to apply the reasonable access and equal opportunities rules to a local cable operator's public access channels since the public, including candidates, already has broad access to such channels.

The broad powers of Congress to regulate interstate commerce should provide adequate constitutional authority for applying political broadcasting rules to cable. Nevertheless, the related First Amendment questions mean the legality of such statutes will always be in doubt until the Supreme Court ultimately decides the issue.

There are several grounds on which the Supreme Court could uphold the applicability of political broadcasting rules to cable. Even without the scarcity justification, the Supreme Court might still uphold the laws as a limited regulation not designed to regulate the actual content of speech, which is nevertheless responding in a reasonable manner to important governmental interests. Or it might see the involvement of the local governmental authority in licensing the cable operator as sufficient state action to require some guarantees of equal access to the facility.[14] Imposition of lowest unit rate rules may be analogous to the long accepted right of state and federal authorities to regulate telephone rates. Until a law is actually enacted and reviewed by the Supreme Court, there is no way to know the precise constitutional limits to the regulation of cable by the country's political broadcasting laws.

---

[13] Of course, CNN as an all-news service may in turn fall under the news exemption to the equal opportunities rules and so in specific cases would not have to grant other candidates equal time. These questions should be decided under the same standards as govern the exemption of programs on commercial TV from the rule's requirements.

[14] See *e.g.* FCC Report to Senator Goldwater, pp. 44-46.

On the other hand, free media proposals are not as appropriate for cable. A cable operator has a responsibility to a particular community as part of its franchise. But the channels that make up the bulk of a cable system's offerings feature uniform national programming, and thus do not lend themselves to free media presentations of local House and Senate candidates. Some of these channels offer nothing but entertainment programming, without any commercial interruption. Free media presentations by House and Senate candidates could therefore appear only on the cable's public access and origination channels. Yet since candidates already have the right to appear free on public access channels (if the candidate asks for time), it would appear unnecessary for the government to impose a free media requirement on these channels as well.

To educate politicians about the possibilities of cable, operators have offered substantial free time to candidates during the last few elections. As one congressional aide described it, "cable operators are trying to look like good public citizens." Local cable operators should do even more in this regard. Just as broadcasters may sponsor debates, or produce programs of their own featuring the candidates, cable operators should use their local origination channels for the same purpose, especially for candidates for the House who may not otherwise be able to obtain time on the air.

The lack of serious time constraints on local origination channels provides an opportunity for cable operators to devote a significant amount of time on these channels to featuring candidates in a variety of formats. Because on many cable systems the origination channels run no programming at all during the majority of hours, presentations featuring candidates on channels would generally not cut into regular programming. Even if the free time provided is not the high *quality* time that candidates and consultants desire most, cable's potential is best tapped as a reliable source of a large *quantity* of time. The audience for these cable presentations would not necessarily be insignificant if candidates combined the presentation with a mailing asking voters to watch.

To increase political programming on cable TV, organizations such as the National Cable Television Association (NCTA) should consider issuing manuals and organizing workshops to promote examination of specific ways cable operators could use their local origination channels for the presentation of candidate interviews, panels, and debates.

If the cable industry granted large quantities of free time to candidates, it would demonstrate that it takes seriously its community obligations. The policy might even be in the economic self-interest of cable operators. If they educated politicians about the medium's potential, they would increase candidates' interest in using cable in later years for paid political advertising.

Radio. Because every market has a large number of radio stations featuring a wide range of formats, it is unnecessary to impose a free media obligation upon every radio station.

Few media markets have more than 10 to 15 broadcast television stations, but nearly every market has many times more radio stations. For example, the Washington, D.C., market — the primary market for five congressional districts — has only four VHF television stations and six UHF television stations but has 26 AM radio stations and 26 FM radio stations. Nationwide, the 435 congressional districts are served by 1,315 television stations but 10,218 radio stations.[15] Thus, free media obligations for all radio stations seem unnecessary and unworkable. In addition, the diversity in programming on radio makes an across-the-board application of free media inappropriate. Listeners might tune in to a sedate "beautiful music" station to find a strident candidate debate, and senatorial candidates would appear on trendy rock stations whose audiences consist largely of non-voting teenagers.

The public trustee standard, however, is as applicable to radio as television. As part of their obligation to the public, radio stations should have a responsibility to devote a significant portion of whatever regular public affairs coverage they already carry to the coverage of elections. Radio stations that provide little news would face a minimal responsibility. "All news" radio stations, on the other hand, should be required to provide candidates opportunities to appear free on the air.

Any free media legislation should direct the FCC to develop guidelines on how much time radio stations should be obligated to provide, based on the station's format. As with television stations, the obligation should be imposed on a per-station rather than a per-candidate basis. Some of the other specifics of the free media proposal suggested in Chapter Four for TV might, however, have to be altered for radio. For example, radio could provide more time than television, and certainly should do it at different times of the day than television.[16]

The recommendations in Chapter Five on lowest unit rate should apply to radio as well as TV.

---

[15] FCC Memorandum Opinion and Order in re Complaint of Syracuse Peace Council against Television Station WTVH, Syracuse, New York, August 4, 1987, p.55.

[16] Prime time for radio, for example, is not the evening but so-called "drive time," between 6 and 9 a.m. and 4 and 7 p.m., when people are in their cars commuting to and from work.

Public Broadcasting. Public television and radio stations should not shoulder the entire burden of free political broadcasting. Their audience is too small to make this an adequate substitute for commercial TV or radio. But neither should public broadcasting be exempted from a free media scheme such as the one outlined in Chapter Four. Because simultaneity is important, and public broadcasting stations are as much public trustees as are commercial stations, public television stations should provide the same amount of free time as commercial stations.

In light of public broadcasting's unique role in producing educational programming, public broadcasting should seek especially to provide programs on House races that might not otherwise be covered by the commercial stations. Public television and radio stations may want to consider ways to use the discretionary funds provided them by the CPB to finance these programs. Another way to finance these programs would be for corporations and nonprofit organizations to become more active in underwriting political programming, an idea discussed in Chapter Seven.

Public television and radio's own organizations should also promote interest among their stations in programs featuring the candidates. Meetings of National Public Radio member stations or the National Association of Public Television Stations should include workshops and other educational programs to educate local stations on topics such as the laws regulating political broadcasting, and ways to encourage candidate appearances. These programs would be particularly useful for public radio stations, which at present appear to play only a minor role in informing the public about congressional candidates.

7.

Steps to Promote Voluntary Airing of Election Programming

> *The broadcast media would be much more willing to involve themselves in informing the public if they weren't so regulated by the government.*
>
> —*A Survey Respondent*

The proposals analyzed in Chapters Four, Five and Six would all impose additional obligations on broadcasters, and increase the regulation of political broadcasting. Yet broadcasters argue that regulation is unnecessary and counterproductive. Some survey respondents strenuously urged removing all regulations on political broadcasting: "I believe in freedom. I do not favor imposing slavery on broadcasters," said one respondent.

This chapter will examine the ways in which current laws may inhibit broadcasters' ability to grant free time, and the ways Congress or federal agencies might remove some of these inhibitions. It will also look at how nonprofit organizations, corporations and labor unions could help make it possible for stations to provide candidates more air time.

1. Repeal of The Equal Opportunities Rule

For over a quarter of a century, broadcasters have attempted to repeal Section 315(a) of the Communications Act, the equal opportunities rule. Congress voted a one-time exemption from equal opportunities for the 1960 general election for President. Congress in 1970 even voted to repeal equal opportunities permanently for all federal elections. As discussed in Chapter Three, that repeal, contained in the 1970 Political Broadcast Act (which also contained an aggregate broadcast spending cap and lowest unit rate), was vetoed by President Nixon. Despite consistent opposition from broadcasters and a 1981 call by the FCC for its repeal, the equal opportunities rule remains in effect.

Broadcasters claim that equal opportunities creates a burdensome obligation. Whenever they feature major party candidates, they must give equal time to all other candidates, even if they are unknown fringe candidates. These concerns may also arise during primaries, if there is a large number of candidates running for the Democratic or Republican nomination. During a primary race, a special program on the leading candidates may require the station to grant equal time to all other primary candidates of the same party. Rather than face subsequent requests for time from the other primary candidates, the argument goes, broadcasters may choose to avoid featuring any of the candidates in the first place.

While several types of programs, including debates, are now exempt from equal opportunities, the obligation may still dissuade broadcasters from producing special programming on candidates in formats which are not exempt from Section 315. For example, specially arranged back-to-back candidate interviews are not exempt from equal opportunities, because they are not regularly scheduled or considered bona fide news events like a debate.

Broadcasters cite anectodal evidence that equal opportunities creates a chilling effect that belies the rule's purpose. For example, when Jesse Jackson appeared on the Phil Donahue show during the 1984 presidential campaign, 130 of the 182 stations that regularly carry the program did not run that particular show out of fears that it would entitle all the other Democratic candidates to equal time.[1] However, anecdotes such as these generally come from presidential races which may feature a multitude of candidates in each party during the primaries.[2]

The detailed political broadcasting data which the FCC collected during the 1960s does not support the claim that the presence of third parties prevents broadcasters from carrying political programming at the congressional level. In 1964, for example, 29 percent of television stations offered free time in the 14 Senate races which were contested by only two candidates; the same percentage of stations offered free time in the 20 multicandidate races.[3] In 1968, the evidence

---

[1] After the program aired, Donahue appealed to the FCC, which held that the appearance qualified for an exemption from Section 315(a) as a regularly scheduled news interview program, thus allowing the program to present candidates in the future without having to provide equal time to all the other candidates.

[2] In a more humorous example of equal opportunities' chilling effect, ABC in 1984 removed outtakes featuring Bozo the Clown from its program "Foul Ups, Bleeps, and Blunders" because Bozo had announced his candidacy for President and the network feared the appearance would trigger requests for equal time. (Bob Packwood, "Equal Access, Equal Opportunities and Chaos," *RTNDA Communicator*, Feb. 1987, p. 6.).

[3] *The Federal Election Campaign Act of 1971: Reform of the Political Process?* 60 Geo. L. J. 1320 (1972). "Free time" in the FCC's study included debate time, which during the 1960s was not exempt from the equal opportunities requirement.

was even more striking: 34 percent of television stations granted free time in two-candidate Senate races; 45 percent gave free time in multicandidate races.

Erwin Krasnow, former Senior Vice President and General Counsel of the NAB and the co-author of *The Politics of Broadcast Regulation*, told the Center that because stations can now broadcast debates, whose confrontational nature makes them the most prevalent and popular free time format, the repeal of Section 315 has become less of a priority among many broadcasters.

Broadcasters nevertheless resent equal opportunities because it implies that they, unlike newspaper publishers, will not treat political candidates fairly. As Roger Colloff, station manager of WCBS-TV in New York, told the Center, "It boils down to saying we cannot be trusted."

As the chart on the following page indicates, the Center's survey found overwhelming opposition to repeal of the equal opportunities rules. Only 16.4 percent of respondents (and only 13.5 percent of winners) either supported or strongly supported a repeal of the law. Those opposing repeal fear that some of the nation's over 1,300 television stations and over 10,000 radio stations would otherwise show undue candidate favoritism. For example, a station could produce a special, half-hour interview of a major party candidate, and provide no air time for his opponent. Not all respondents agreed. As one candidate said, "Stations should be allowed to do what they want to do. There is enough competition to motivate broadcasters to act as good citizens."[4]

2. Third Parties and the Equal Opportunities Rule

Any chilling effect the equal opportunities rule may havem on stations need not cause outright repeal of the law. Instead, the rule's applicability to third parties could be limited. Broadcasters could then air presentations of major party candidates without having to provide equal time to all third party candidates.

One way to accomplish this would be to enact legislation broadening the existing exemptions to the equal opportunities rule. For example, one petition denied in 1988 by the FCC proposed to treat as news programming exempt from the equal time rule any joint or back-to-back appearances of candidates, as well as "any program in which the content, format, and participants are determined by the licensee or network and which is bona fide in nature, i.e., designed to contribute to an informed electorate and not to serve

---

[4] When broadcaster bias does occur, it may take the form of a helping hand rather than a negative attack. One candidate in the survey told the Center, "Our area broadcasters were very supportive of our efforts and helped us out with the big spot (a five-minute ad produced by the campaign) from a time selection and production aspect."

Views of Survey Respondents on Proposals to Abolish the Equal Opportunities Doctrine

Question:

"How does your candidate feel about the following: Repeal the equal time doctrine which requires broadcasters to offer comparable time at comparable rates to all candidates, if it is offered to one candidate?"

Overall

Strongly Oppose	31.8%
Oppose	39.4%
No Opinion	12.4%
Support	7.6%
Strongly Support	8.8%

By Winners/Losers

	Winners	Losers
Strongly Oppose	28.1%	35.8%
Oppose	42.7%	35.8%
No Opinion	15.7%	8.6%
Support	5.6%	9.9%
Strongly Support	7.9%	9.9%

By Chamber

	House	Senate
Strongly Oppose	32.4%	29.4%
Oppose	40.4%	35.3%
No Opinion	8.8%	26.5%
Support	8.1%	5.9%
Strongly Support	10.3%	2.9%

By Party

	Democrats	Republicans
Strongly Oppose	46.3%	18.9%
Oppose	36.3%	42.2%
No Opinion	11.3%	13.3%
Support	5.0%	10.0%
Strongly Support	1.3%	15.6%

Source: Center for Responsive Politics

the political advantage of any candidate."[5] This exemption would allow broadcasters to produce in-depth candidate interviews, back-to-back presentations of the candidates, special documentaries on the campaign, or a general discussion of election issues, without incurring any obligation to other candidates under the equal opportunities rule.

While expanding the news exemption would negate most remaining concerns about third party candidates, other proposals eliminate these concerns by directly restricting the law's applicability to third party candidates.

Strong national third party efforts are usually driven by the strength of a single personality running for President. They rarely possess the grass-roots organization capable of mounting successful congressional races across the country. The practical problem in House and Senate races is, therefore, not how to treat these strong third party efforts, but rather how to handle the proliferation of congressional candidates from fringe parties. As the charts on the following pages indicate, in 1986 a total of 144 third party candidates from fringe parties ran in 117 of the 435 congressional districts, while a total of 28 third party candidates ran in 15 of the 33 states with Senate races. Of these 172 candidates, only five outside of New York (where the Liberal and Conservative parties are long established) ever exceeded 1 percent of the vote. None of the Senate candidates, and only 3 House candidates outside of New York, received over 2 percent of the vote.

With perhaps these conditions in mind, Sen. Albert Gore, Sr. (D-TN) in 1970 introduced a bill that would have made the equal opportunities requirement applicable only to candidates of parties that garnered two percent of the vote in the last election, or that had submitted petitions equal to one percent of the vote for that office in the last election.[6] Other candidates would have been covered by the Fairness Doctrine.

---

[5] Henry Geller, Donna Lampert, Petition of the WEBE-108 Radio Company L.P. before the FCC, February 19, 1987. The petition was submitted to the FCC by a station wishing to feature major party Presidential candidates on its programs.

[6] Although the constitutionality of such a law may be open to attack, the Supreme Court has shown considerable willingness to uphold reasonable distinctions between major and minor parties in federal elections law. The Court has held that there are differences in kind between major and minor parties, and observed that sometimes the grossest discrimination can lie in treating things that are different as though they were exactly alike. Jenness v. Fortson, 403 U.S. 431, 441-442 (1971); Buckley v. Valeo, 424 U.S. at 97. In American Party of Texas v. White, 415 U.S. 767, 794 (1974), the Court observed that the Constitution does not require the government to "finance the effort of every nascent political group."

Third Parties in the 1986 House Elections

State	# of districts with third party candidates	Total # of third party candidates	# of candidates above 1%	# of candidates above 2%
Alabama	1 of 7	1		
Alaska	1 of 1	1		
Arizona	1 of 5	1		
Arkansas	1 of 4	1		
California	30 of 45	38		
Colorado	1 of 6	1		
Connecticut	0 of 6	0		
Delaware	1 of 1	1		
Florida	0 of 19	0		
Georgia	0 of 10	0		
Hawaii	2 of 2	2		
Idaho	1 of 2	1		
Illinois	1 of 22	1		
Indiana	4 of 10	5		
Iowa	0 of 6	0		
Kansas	0 of 5	0		
Kentucky	2 of 7	3		
Maine	1 of 2	1	1	1
Maryland	0 of 8	0		
Massachusetts	0 of 11	0		
Michigan	8 of 17	10		
Minnesota	2 of 8	2		
Mississippi	0 of 5	0		
Missouri	1 of 9	1		
Montana	0 of 2	0		
Nebraska	0 of 3	0		

Continued on next page

Third Parties in the 1986 House Elections *(continued)*

State	# of districts with third party candidates	Total # of third party candidates	# of candidates above 1%	# of candidates above 2%
Nevada	1 of 2	1		
New Hampshire	0 of 2	0		
New Jersey	6 of 14	9		
New Mexico	0 of 3	0		
New York	22 of 34	26	24	21
North Carolina	0 of 11	0		
North Dakota	1 of 1	1		
Ohio	4 of 21	4		
Oklahoma	1 of 6	1		
Oregon	0 of 5	0		
Pennsylvania	4 of 23	7	1	1
Rhode Island	0 of 2	0		
South Carolina	1 of 6	1		
South Dakota	0 of 1	0		
Tennessee	2 of 9	4		
Texas	7 of 27	7		
Utah	2 of 3	3		
Vermont	1 of 1	3	1	1
Virginia	3 of 10	3		
Washington	0 of 8	0		
West Virginia	0 of 4	0		
Wisconsin	4 of 9	4		
Wyoming	0 of 1	0		
Totals	**117 of 435**	**144**	**127**	**24**

Source: *1986 Congressional Quarterly Almanac*

Third Parties in the 1986 Senate Elections

State	# of Third Party candidates	Candidates receiving 1% or more
Alabama	0	
Alaska	1	
Arizona	0	
Arkansas	0	
California	3	
Colorado	4	
Connecticut	0	
Florida	0	
Georgia	0	
Hawaii	0	
Idaho	0	
Indiana	2	
Iowa	1	
Kansas	0	
Kentucky	0	
Louisiana	0	
Maryland	0	
Missouri	0	
Nevada	1	
New Hampshire	1	
New York	3	John Dyson (Liberal), 2%
North Carolina	0	
North Dakota	1	Anne Bourgois (Independent), 1%
Ohio	0	
Oklahoma	0	
Oregon	0	
Pennsylvania	1	
South Carolina	2	
South Dakota	0	
Utah	2	
Vermont	2	Anthony Doria (Conservative), 2%
Washington	1	
Wisconsin	3	
Totals	**28**	**3 candidates**

Source: *1986 Congressional Quarterly Almanac*

Another way suggested by some scholars to filter out fringe parties would be to ask all candidates wishing to use the equal opportunities rule to post bond. The bond would be in the amount of a certain high percentage of the cost of the broadcast time, and it would be forfeited to the broadcaster if the candidate did not achieve a certain minimal level of the popular vote. Because only candidates who expect to fare well in the election could afford to post the money, it would select out the frivolous candidates, yet leave the door open for emerging parties.[7]

3. Debates and the Equal Opportunities Rule

Debates have become an attractive way for stations to give political candidates air time outside of news programs which is nevertheless exempt from the equal opportunities rules.[8] Because stations can only air debates in a general election if both major party candidates agree to appear, debates frequently do not occur when one candidate chooses not to participate. This section will examine how candidates, rather than stations, can prevent a proposed debate from taking place, and how a modification of the equal opportunities rule might encourage candidates to debate.

Frequency of Congressional Debates. While there are no records publicly available indicating how many debates were held in the 1986 election, the Center's survey discovered them to be commonplace. In 1986, 72.7 percent said they received at least one offer to participate in a debate to be broadcast on the air. During the general election, 65.6% of those receiving offers said the debate took place. These figures seem in line with a survey by the NAB of 303 television stations immediately after the 1986 elections. It found that over 56.1 percent of the stations surveyed offered free debate time to candidates for *some* local, state, or federal office, and 46.2 percent of all stations aired at least one debate.[9]

---

[7] Howard Penniman and Ralph Winter, Jr., *Campaign Finances: The Views of the Political and Constitutional Implications*, Washington D.C., American Enterprise Institute, 1971, p. 69.

[8] As discussed in Chapter Three, broadcasters obtained large exemptions to equal opportunities in FCC's Aspen and League of Women Voters rulings of 1975 and 1983. The first ruling allowed broadcasters to air debates, so long as the debate was staged by an outside organization. Broadcasters could cover these debates, generally sponsored by groups such as the League of Women Voters, as newsworthy events. The second ruling created another exemption, allowing broadcasters to organize their own debates. These exemptions allow stations to feature the major party candidates in debates without having to provide time to third party candidates.

[9] *Political Air time '86, Summary of Survey Results Conducted for NAB by National Research, Inc,* NAB Public Affairs and Communications, 1986.

The League of Women Voters, in its 1986 "Agenda for Security" project, sponsored debates in 16 Senate and 50 House races, including most of the hotly contested races of the year, to focus attention on national security and nuclear war issues.[10] The League estimates that 1986 Agenda for Security debates were seen by 2.4 million households; 1.6 million for 16 Senate debates (one in every ten voters in these states) and 800,000 for the 50 House debates. Though debates featuring close Senate races received prime-time coverage, many House races were broadcast during less favorable times, such as Sunday morning.[11] The League selected its races based upon the significance of the contest, the quality of the debate plans produced by local Leagues, and geographic diversity.

In a survey sponsored by the League of Women Voters in connection with its program, broadcasters indicated they "were interested in airing debates in order to improve their public service image," and were particularly interested in airing debates in tight races.[12] In all, the League estimates that in connection with League-sponsored events, broadcasters donated $300,000 of free commercial air time, and at least another $300,000 to cover production-related expenses.

The Value of Debates to Candidates. The Center's survey revealed that candidates who chose to debate generally found it to be a positive experience for their campaigns. An overwhelming 72.4 percent of respondents said that the debate helped their campaign, while only 17.3 percent felt that it had not. While 91.7 percent of challengers believed that debates helped them, 60.0 percent of incumbents also felt that debates had helped their campaign.

Candidates in the Center's survey found debates useful for varying reasons. To challengers, debates sometimes offered their only real media exposure. One respondent believed his candidacy was helped because, as he succinctly put it, "I was not the incumbent, I was behind in the polls. I won the

---

[10] League of Women Voters Education Fund, *Agenda for Security, Debates '86, Final Report*, Washington D.C., 1987, p. 11. In arranging these debates, the LWVEF, a §501(c)(3) tax exempt organization, gave small grants to local Leagues to use in the planning of the debates. The local Leagues, which are §501(c)(4) tax exempt organizations, planned the debate, helped make arrangements, handled negotiations with broadcasters, and worked with broadcasters in publicizing the debate.

[11] Of the League's 16 Senate election debates, 13 were broadcast on commercial affiliates and three were broadcast on public television stations. Of the House debates, 24 aired on commercial stations, 15 on public television, 10 on cable and one on radio.

[12] League of Women Voters Education Fund, *Agenda for Security. Debates '86, Final Report*, p. 11.

debate." Many were simply confident that the debate allowed the public to become familiar with the issues, making such comments as, "I clearly won the debate on the issues," and "[debates] gave me an opportunity to show that I knew about the issues and that my opponent did not." One Republican Senate candidate found debates beneficial for the substantive message they conveyed: "I was perceived as a strong Reaganite, a clone of the President. The debate established areas where I was different from the President." Another had a more whimsical opinion of the effectiveness of debates: "The debate didn't help anybody but it did put several sleep aid companies out of business."

Indicative of the respondents' generally favorable attitude towards debates was their response to the question whether any free media law adopted should require broadcasters to provide some of the time for debates. Results of the Center's survey indicated 58.5 percent favored this, including 72.1 percent of challengers.

Although candidates generally had a favorable opinion of debates, their occurrence depends on the cooperation of both candidates and the media. And because candidates in the lead are often unwilling to help their opponents gain exposure, debates often do not occur.

The Center's survey found that 22.7 percent of candidates said they had declined on at least one occasion to participate in a broadcast debate in 1986. Confirming the hypothesis that incumbents turn down debates more than challengers, 39.0 percent of incumbents said they had declined a debate, while only 5.9 percent of challengers ever declined a debate offer.

Furthermore, the Center's survey revealed that debates were more likely to occur when a race was close. In noncompetitive races (where the winner received over 60 percent of the vote), 64.2 percent of proposed debates actually took place, while in competitive races (where the winner received less than 60 percent of the vote), 86.8 percent of the proposed debates actually occurred. Broadcasters were also more willing to offer debates when a race was highly competitive. Debates were offered to 88.6 percent of the survey respondents in competitive races, but only 66.4 percent of candidates in noncompetitive races.

The 1986 NAB study of broadcast stations also indicated that many debates never take place. In the case of 45.3 percent of those stations offering debates, at least *one* debate proposed by the station never occurred (on any level, federal, state or local elections) because one or both of the candidates did not accept the offer. It should be noted that, because the same stations could have made several debate offers which *were* accepted, it is impossible to determine from the NAB's numbers precisely what percentage of debates proposed actually occurred.

Respondents to the Center's survey proved forthcoming in explaining why they accepted or declined debate proposals. Most of the challengers accepted debate invitations. Typical of their answers was one who explained, "I was the underdog in the campaign. Airtime would only help me." Most incumbents who turned down debate invitations cited scheduling conflicts: "Schedule conflicts with Congress in session"; "We backed out the last minute because he had a House vote"; "Heavy schedule demands elsewhere." Only a few actually stated that they turned down the debate for reasons of political strategy. As one said, "Yes, I refused. My political judgment was that debating is not helpful to the incumbent."

The League of Women Voters similarly reported that some candidates engaged in endless discussions over the date, format, or site of the debate in the hopes that the League sponsor would abandon the effort. To counter these efforts, Leagues generally took their case to the press, announcing major developments in their negotiations as they occurred.[13] In California they even arranged a postcard campaign and aired commercials with Hollywood actors urging the Senate candidates to debate. Because the League recognized that broadcasters are more likely to carry Senate races and extremely high profile House races, local Leagues offered trade-offs for broadcasters which wanted to air high-profile Senate debates. In Philadelphia, the League offered to stage a debate in the heated Bob Edgar-Arlen Specter Senate race only if the station airing the debate also agreed to air three local House debates. The League convinced KUSA (CBS) in Denver to accept a similar arrangement — the Senate debate came only in a package with five House debates.

Proposals to Encourage Debates. To encourage candidates to accept debate offers, it is necessary to change incumbents' strategic equation. A relatively limited adjustment in the equal opportunities rules could help do this.

Currently, if a broadcaster offers debate time to both major candidates and one candidate declines, the debate exemption would not be available to the station. If the station went ahead with a program featuring the candidate who had accepted the offer to debate, it would have to offer equal time to the other candidate on another occasion. A 1978 FCC advisory letter stated that the equal opportunities exemption for debates is contingent upon "the confrontation

---

[13] One survey respondent provided an example of the lengths to which candidates themselves will go to generate unfavorable public reaction against a candidate who declines to debate. An empty chair debate actually occurred in this respondent's race, only the chair was not entirely empty — it was filled with a dummy of his opponent. Said the candidate's campaign manager, "The candidate rented a hall and invited his opponent to debate. When his opponent refused, the candidate had the debate (with the dummy) filmed. This film was shown on several stations."

between opposing candidates in a debate format or other joint appearance. Without this face-to-face meeting, an appearance by a candidate cannot come within the exemption in the *Aspen* decision."[14] The broadcaster will therefore generally cancel the program if one candidate declines to participate, in order to avoid equal opportunities obligations to the non-participant and to any third party candidates.

To encourage front-runners to debate, broadcasters who organize a debate could be allowed to air the program even if only one of the candidates chooses to participate, without having to provide equal time later to the candidates who declined to debate, or to any third party candidates. Presumably the station would not stage a debate with an empty chair, but would instead present the cooperating candidate in an interview or other, more innovative format. This exemption might increase the number of debates held, because candidates could not deny their opponents air time by refusing to participate in the debate.

This approach might create several problems unless carefully limited. First, it could undermine the intent of equal opportunities by opening the door to broadcaster favoritism. Broadcasters could embarrass a candidate by scheduling a debate for an inconvenient time (e.g., at a time when an incumbent has congressional business in Washington).

Second, even if broadcasters received this exemption, they might not be interested in airing a special program featuring only one of the candidates. Some stations might instead choose to arrange for the interested candidate to appear on a regularly scheduled news interview program, making any change in the current rules unnecessary. Other stations might be inclined to cancel the candidate's appearance altogether because without both candidates the program would lack compelling interest, and might create a public impression of one-sidedness. Whereas a debate would likely be newsworthy enough to trigger stories in local newscasts and the following day's newspaper, such an interview would probably generate less news coverage. Indeed, what often makes debates influential is not the perception of voters watching the debate — viewership can be minuscule — but rather how the press interprets the candidates' comparative performance. Some survey respondents took note of this phenomenon: "The debate didn't matter," explained one incumbent, "but the news coverage of the debate did matter."

Recognizing these realities, the candidate reluctant to debate might still turn down the invitation even if his or her opponent were entitled to free time. A refusal to debate would not hurt the candidate because either the broadcaster would

---

[14] Letter from Arthur L. Ginsburg, Acting Chief, Complaints and Compliance Division, FCC Broadcast Bureau, to Mr. M. Robert Rogers, President, Radio Station WANV, April 21, 1978.

cancel the event, or comparatively few voters would bother to watch the "empty chair debate" or interview program.

Nevertheless, of all the proposals for reform in the Center's survey, the expansion of the debate exemption proved the most popular among respondents. Of those surveyed, 61 percent either supported or strongly supported permitting stations an exemption from the equal opportunities rules even if only one candidate accepted an invitation to debate. Only 27.2 percent opposed or strongly opposed it. The proposal even carried a plurality among incumbents — 39.2 percent to 37.9 percent — though it was especially popular among challengers (85.5 percent to 11.5 percent).

4. The Federal Election Laws and Donations of Free Time by Stations

Aside from providing time for debates, stations may wish to provide candidates with free broadcast time to use as they wish. However, they may be reluctant to do so because of uncertainty over whether such a grant of free time represents a corporate contribution prohibited by the federal election laws.

In September 1986, Rep. Howard Coble (R-NC) asked the FEC if he could accept a Greensboro station's offer of free time to air commercials. WGGT-TV made the offer to both Rep. Coble and his Democratic opponent, Robin Britt, who was attempting to recapture the seat he lost to Coble in 1984. The station offered free of charge eighteen 30-second public service slots to both major party candidates to increase voter awareness.

The FEC originally told Rep. Coble's campaign committee in an advisory opinion that the television station would be violating the law's strict ban on corporate contributions, which includes gifts of "anything of value." In this case, broadcast time for commercials, which would otherwise be sold to the candidates, represented something of value.[15]

The NAB asked the FEC to reconsider its initial opinion. In its request, the NAB stated that the FEC's decision "appears to contravene Congress' mandate" in two provisions of the Communications Act, reasonable access and equal opportunities. The NAB pointed out that FEC regulations exempt from the definition of a campaign contribution any "cost incurred in covering or carrying a news story, commentary, or editorial by any broadcasting station . . . unless the facility is owned or controlled by any political party, political committee, or candidate."[16] Citing various earlier opinions by the FEC, the NAB argued that

---

[15] FEC Advisory Opinion 1986-35.
[16] 11 CFR §100.7(b)(2).

WGGT's offer should fall under this exemption because "providing free time directly to candidates on a nonpartisan basis is . . . a legitimate press function."[17]

In addition, Section 312(a)(7), the reasonable access law, can be read as encouraging broadcasters to give candidates free media time because it gives the FCC authority to revoke a station license for

> willful or repeated failure to allow reasonable access to *or to permit purchase of* reasonable amounts of time for use of the broadcasting station by a legally qualified candidate for Federal elective office on behalf of his candidacy. [Emphasis added.]

This wording implies that stations have a choice between making either paid or free time available to candidates in fulfilling their reasonable access obligations.

The Commission agreed after the election to reconsider its decision in the WGGT-TV ruling. Though Republican Commissioner Thomas Josefiak's motion to reissue the original opinion in a slightly modified form was originally passed by a 4-2 margin, Republican Commissioner Joan Aikens later switched her vote to create a 3-3 deadlock. This left the earlier opinion vacated without a new opinion to replace it. The FEC's action means that the apparent conflict between the FEC and FCC laws remains unresolved, thereby discouraging any broadcaster from voluntarily making available free time that the candidate would otherwise have to purchase.

The Center's survey revealed that several candidates may, in fact, have received offers of free time in 1986. A total of 14.7 percent said they had been offered some type of free broadcast time, other than debates, newscasts or news interview programs. Although some who said they had been offered such time cited radio talk shows, in other cases respondents said they had received free commercial time. One candidate received free "three-minute spots to say whatever I wanted to say. Four or five radio stations offered these three-minute spots." Another candidate told the Center, "Both candidates were offered 13 free radio

---

[17] National Association of Broadcasters' letter to Joan D. Aikens, Chairman, October 20, 1986. In 1982, the FEC held in AO 1982-44 that the offer of Atlanta's superstation WTBS (TV) of two-hour blocks of time to both the Democratic and Republican national committees fell under this commentary exemption. In another, similar case, former Rep. Robert Duncan (D-OR) produced a film with campaign funds which depicted facilities available to constituents and services provided by his congressional office. The FEC ruled in AO 1978-76 that a television station could run the spots free of charge after the election under the "news story, commentary, or editorial" exemption.

spots." These offers almost certainly represented "something of value" because the candidate would otherwise have had to purchase the time.

Respondents to the Center's survey split evenly on the desirability of legislation to clarify the election law in this area. Results showed 42.9 percent either supported or strongly supported such legislation, while 42.9 percent opposed or strongly opposed it.[18]

5. The Role of Corporations, Labor Unions and Nonprofit Organizations In Providing Airtime for Candidates

Current law allows nonprofit organizations, corporations and labor unions to work with stations in promoting media appearances by candidates. Whether or not mandatory free media requirements are adopted, the involvement of these organizations could increase the number of debates and other political programs a station carries.

Although broadcasters now stage some debates themselves, others continue to be organized by public charities exempt from taxes under Section 501 (c)(3) or Section 501 (c)(4) of the Internal Revenue Code.

Public charities exempt from tax under these provisions may not participate in or intervene in any political campaign in support of, or in opposition to, any candidate for public office.[19] As demonstrated by the activities of the League of Women Voters, however, public charities can sponsor certain debates without violating these restrictions. The Internal Revenue Service has repeatedly found that the conduct of public forums involving qualified candidates for public office does not constitute participation or intervention in a political campaign, so long as the debates are carried on in a nonpartisan manner.

In a recent ruling, the IRS concluded that "A forum held for the purpose of educating and informing the voters, which provides fair and impartial treatment of candidates, and which does not promote or advance one candidate over another, would not constitute participation or intervention in any political campaign on behalf of or in opposition to any candidate for public office."[20]

---

[18] In the 100th Congress, Rep. Swift's H.R. 2464.addressed a similar issue The bill would allow newspapers to provide free newspaper space at their discretion to candidates without it being considered a corporate contribution.

[19] I.R.C. §501(c)(3) and see Treas. Reg. 1.501(c)(4)-1(a)(2)(ii). While neither type of organization may participate in political campaigns, a section 501 (c)(4) organization has greater freedom to lobby and to communicate with its members than does a 501(c)(3) organization.

[20] Rev. Rul. 86-95, 1986-2 C.B. 73; see also Rev. Rul. 66-256, 1966-2 C.B. 210.

Indications that a forum is being conducted in a permissible manner include invitations to all legally qualified candidates; use of a nonpartisan independent expert panel to question the candidates; adoption of a method for assuring that each candidate has an equal opportunity to respond; selection of a moderator whose sole function is to enforce the ground rules; and statements that the candidates' views are not those of the organization.[21]

Special rules apply to the portion of tax-exempt organizations that operate as private foundations. These rules would not prevent private foundations from funding public charities of the type described above who are interested in sponsoring a debate. Under the tax code, private foundations are barred from expending funds, "to influence the outcome of any specific public election or to carry on, directly or indirectly, any voter registration drive."[22] Providing funding for a debate should not, however, run afoul of this prohibition. The IRS regulatory definition of what constitutes influencing the outcome of a specific public election by a private foundation is very similar to the statutory prohibition on political campaign activities applicable to all Section 501(c)(3) organizations. The regulation prohibits foundations from participating or intervening, directly or indirectly, "in any political campaign on behalf of or in opposition to any candidate for public office."[23] Since sponsoring nonpartisan debates does not constitute participation or intervention in a political campaign in violation of Section 501(c)(3), foundations may also make grants to public charities to sponsor candidate debates.[24]

Corporations and labor unions can play a role too. Current FEC regulations permit a corporation or labor union to donate money to nonprofit educational organizations, such as the League of Women Voters, to stage

---

[21] Rev. Rul. 86-95, 1986-2C.B. 73.

[22] I.R.C. §4945(d)(2). An exception to this prohibition is provided for support for certain organizations carrying on nonpartisan activities in five or more states and over more than one election period. I.R.C. §4945(f). This exception permits foundations to provide grants to certain organizations to carry on voter registration drives.

[23] Treas. Reg. §53.4945-3(a)(2).

[24] A grant by a private foundation directly to a broadcaster which is not a tax-exempt organization would require the foundation to exercise close supervision to ensure that the money is expended in nonpolitical ways in compliance with the law. Since most foundations are reluctant to assume this responsibility, a foundation would prefer to make grants to a public charity to enable the charity to in turn sponsor the debate.

debates.[25] To qualify, a corporation or labor union may provide funds only to a nonprofit organization that does not in the debate "endorse, support or oppose political candidates or political parties." The FEC also requires that the organization receiving the funds must be exempt from taxes under Section 501 (c) (3) or Section 501 (c) (4) of the Tax Code.

Although the law is not entirely clear, the FEC currently takes a restrictive view of any more direct corporate or labor union involvement in political programming. Generally, it prohibits direct sponsorship of programs featuring the candidates, except in those unusual instances when it believes safeguards fully prevent the corporation or labor union from exercising any partisan control over the program's content.[26] As a result, the Commission usually interprets current law as prohibiting a corporation or labor union from offering to buy all the commerical time on a special program featuring candidates for federal office. The FEC is likely to be concerned that the donor, by initiating and financing such programming, would exercise control over the program's timing or format, and thereby violate the prohibition against corporate or labor union contributions made for the purpose of influencing any federal office.

6. Recommendations

To encourage broadcasters to increase voluntarily the amount of air time they provide candidates, the Center recommends the following:

- The equal opportunities doctrine should not be repealed, but should be amended by limiting its applicability to major candidates (major parties and third parties that receive more than 2 percent of the votes).

---

[25] 11CFR §114.4(e)(3). The regulation states: "A corporation or labor organization may donate funds to nonprofit organizations qualified under 11 CFR 110.13(a)(1) to stage nonpartisan candidate debates held in accordance with 11 CFR 110.13 and 114.4(e)."

[26] The following illustrates the narrow circumstances when FEC might approve such involvement: In 1987, the American International Group, Inc. (AIG), proposed to sponsor a thirteen-week interview series with presidential candidates hosted by David Frost, and produced by the magazine, *U.S. News and World Report*. AIG would not control or participate in the production or distribution of the series, the selection of the candidates, or the timing of the series in different markets. The corporation would merely pay a sponsorship fee for advertisements on these syndicated programs, but would not be the sole advertiser. Because of these circumstances, the Commission ruled that AIG's sponsorship of the series would not represent a corporate contribution. The Commission also concluded that *U.S. News'* activity fell under the news story exemption in 2 U.S.C. 431 (9)(B)(i) and therefore would not result in a contribution from *U.S. News* to the candidates. See FEC Advisory Opinion 1987-88, May 4, 1987.

- Congress should also expand the news exemption to include joint or back-to-back appearances of candidates.

- A limited exemption from the equal opportunities rule should be available to a station willing to air a debate, even if one of the candidates declines to participate in the debate.

- Congress should clarify that the prohibition in federal election laws against corporate contributions does not prohibit media companies from donating free air time to candidates, so long as all major candidates in the race receive equal time.

- The election laws governing general corporate or labor union sponsorship of debates should be clarified in order that they may become more directly involved in sponsoring debates and other informative election programming, so long as the station maintains full editorial control.

- Private foundations, corporations and labor unions should increase their funding of public charities working to promote debates between candidates.

- The FCC should resume collecting data on the amount of special election programming each radio and television station airs during the election period.

Whether or not Congress enacts a mandatory free media law, Congress and the FCC should take every step to encourage voluntary efforts by stations that would increase free appearances of candidates on the air. These steps would test the accuracy of broadcasters' claims that stations would substantially increase coverage of candidates if regulatory restrictions were removed. They would also avoid the rigidity and complexity that could come to characterize a mandatory free media program.

The following, therefore, details a number of steps that might increase the amount of free time stations voluntarily provide candidates.

Equal Time. A full repeal of Section 315 does not seem either desirable or — given the Center's survey results — politically likely. Complete repeal of the equal opportunities rule would entrust station managers with the power to determine which candidates would receive air time. While most stations would be scrupulously fair to both candidates, there is always the chance a few would abuse their position to favor one candidate over another. Furthermore, it is unnecessary to repeal the equal opportunitites rule just to address the third party problem. As we have seen, only a limited number of third parties receive a significant number of votes for Congress. It would be more constructive to preserve the equal opportunities principle, yet remove the most chilling aspects of the current law.

Congress should therefore enact legislation limiting the equal opportunities law to only major party candidates and significant third parties. This would allow stations to air major candidates in any format, whether or not the program happened to fit under one of the exemptions from the equal opportunities rule. So long as broadcasters featured equal appearances of all major party candidates and all significant third party candidates, they would not have to grant equal time to other third party candidates. The legislation should define "significant" third parties at a reasonable level. For example, this might mean any party that received more than two percent of the vote in the last general election, or that can obtain petition signatures from two percent of the voters in the last election.

In 1986, a two percent threshhold would have excluded all but 24 third party candidates in congressional races out of a total of 144 third party candidates that ran for Congress. Of the 24, a total of 21 came from the New York City area, where the Liberal, Conservative, and Right-to-Life parties field candidates in most congressional districts. Even lowering the threshhold to one percent would only include three congressional candidates outside of New York and three additional candidates in the New York area. This new standard thus would preserve the equal opportunities doctrine for any significant third party candidates, yet in almost all races reduce any tendency of the current law to inhibit innovative programming by broadcasters.

Whether or not such legislation is enacted, the Center recommends that Congress expand the exemption for coverage of bona fide news events to include joint or back-to-back presentations by all major candidates. This proposal would allow broadcasters to feature candidates in these formats without having to provide equal time to third party candidates. The rationale for this change is very simple: joint or back-to-back appearances of the candidates can hardly be distinguished conceptually from in-studio debates, which are already exempted. Stations should not have to hold an actual "debate" if they wish to produce a program featuring two or more candidates on the air.

This approach would help address the broadcasters' concerns with third party candidates, even if the equal opportunities rule as a whole was not amended to apply only to candidates of parties receiving over two percent of the vote. In one respect, it would address the issue more effectively than enactment of a two percent threshold. If this threshold were adopted, a station would still have to give equal time to all major party candidates that enter a primary, no matter how numerous. Exempting joint or back-to-back appearances from the equal opportunities rule would enable broadcasters in primary elections to exclude fringe candidates from such programs if the station, in its editorial discretion, felt it necessary.

Overall, both of these changes to the equal opportunites rule would encourage stations to give candidates a greater opportunity to present their views on the air, and make stations more likely to present innovative, informative election programming.

Appearances When One Candidate Declines to Debate. As discussed above, many stations are thwarted in their efforts to air debates because candidates who are ahead choose not to give their opponents additional exposure.

A modification in the equal opportunities rule permitting broadcasters to air a program exempt from the equal opportunities rule even if one candidate declines to participate would address this problem. The station or other sponsor should not be obligated to stage a literal debate with an empty chair, but could present the participating candidate in any format the station chose. Today, a station unable to arrange a debate may put candidates on regularly scheduled news interview shows that are exempt from the equal opportunities rule. But these programs are generally scheduled in light viewing hours and have a static format. This change in the law would enable stations to schedule special programs different in format from the normal interview show and during prime time when they would attract more viewers.

To guard against possible abuse, a station should be allowed to invoke this exemption from the equal opportunities rule only once for each race, and only if no other debate between the candidates had been aired already by another station. Furthermore, a station would not be entitled to the exemption if the FCC determined upon a complaint by the other candidate that the station or sponsor had not made a reasonable effort to arrange the debate at a convenient time, and in an equitable format. Should the FCC conclude that the station did not make a reasonable offer, the other candidate would be entitled to equal time.

The Center believes this change would represent a measured way to encourage candidates to debate their opponents.

Contributions of Free Broadcast Time by Station. The Federal Election Commission or Congress should clarify the election laws in order to permit stations to provide free air time to candidates without it being considered a corporate contribution. So that stations do not abuse this right in order to help one candidate over another, the equal opportunities law would apply to any free time donated.[27] With the equal opportunities safeguard in place, there would seem to be no need for the election law's ban on donations of free time to candidates.

Sponsorship of Candidate Appearances by Corporations, Labor Unions and Foundations. If more private organizations became involved in sponsoring political programming, more federal candidates would receive free air time, making imposition of a mandatory free media requirement less necessary. Corporations, labor unions and private foundations should all play a larger role in this process.

Restricting corporations and labor unions to funding only debates organized by nonprofit groups was logical when only nonprofits, rather than broadcasters, could stage debates. Now that broadcasters can also stage debates, there seems little reason that corporations and labor unions should not be able to fund more directly debates staged by a station. Such funding would allow stations to sponsor debates or other special political programming without sacrificing revenues.

The FEC should adjust its regulations accordingly to encourage such increased activity by labor unions and corporations. To ensure against abuse, corporate or labor union involvement could be limited to debates, or back-to-back or joint appearances of the type described in section two of this chapter. The regulations should further specify that the arrangement between corporations and labor unions and broadcasters must parallel the relationship now permitted between corporations or labor unions and nonprofits. As with League of Women Voters debates, the donor would retain no control over the specific content or format of the program, which would be produced under the sole direction of the station. The donor would merely provide funds for the debate by agreeing to buy all commercial time on the program.

Corporations or labor unions, if they are reluctant to fund debates directly for fear of offending an incumbent important to their interests, or for other reasons, should contribute in larger amounts to nonprofit organizations sponsoring debates. This too would have the effect of increasing the amount of election programming aired.

Private foundations can also play a valuable role in political broadcasting. They should find greater opportunities to promote an informed electorate by funding nonprofit educational groups working to promote media coverage of congressional races. The experience of the League of Women Voters

---

[27] Since print media are not subject to similar equal opportunities restraints, a different and perhaps more difficult question would arise as to how to apply this rule to any form of media not subject to Section 315 or its equivalent.

demonstrates that, once funded, these nonprofit groups can employ innovative techniques to convince stations to broadcast debates and to bring public pressure on candidates who express reluctance to debate.

Community foundations active at the state or local level should consider playing a funding role in this area as well since congressional candidates run at the state or local level, and no national foundation could have the resources to fund programs in all congressional districts and Senate races.

FCC Record Keeping. Finally, in order to gauge whether further changes in the political broadcasting laws are necessary, the FCC should resume collecting data on political broadcasting from all stations, as it did from 1956 to 1973.

In these reports, the FCC should compile data on the amount of free time, debates and other special political programming that radio and television stations aired during the election period. All of this information is readily accessible to each licensee.

Such reports would constitute a record which the FCC could consult when determining, at the time the station's license is up for renewal, whether the station fulfilled its public interest obligations as a licensee.

8.

Democracy and the Electronic Media

A society such as ours, which seeks to govern itself as a democracy, must value highly all forms of political speech. Without it, this country's political system cannot operate. The critical role of campaigns in America's democratic system requires that the candidates for federal office receive a full and fair hearing.

In our electronic age, a full and fair hearing can only occur if both candidates have an opportunity to discuss the issues on the air. Congress recognized this three decades ago in a report accompanying amendments to the equal opportunities rule:

> Broadcasting and in particular television today is the most powerful medium of communications available to candidates for public office . . . It has an unusual potential to sharpen the public interest in and knowledge of political life . . . Every means must be taken to bring to as many people as possible the views of the candidates. Only then is the viewer in a position to form an intelligent opinion as to whom to select to lead the Nation in this critical period.[1]

Today, the American political broadcasting system is virtually unique among the major democracies in relying on paid advertisements, rather than providing free air time for candidates to express their views. As a result, the American electoral system has also become unique in other ways — in its level of campaign spending, in the time candidates must spend raising money, and in the influence of 30-second spots.

At present, the high cost of air time represents a significant barrier to free speech during campaigns. It also throws up other, less obvious, barriers. The current electoral system forces candidates to spend too much of their time raising money, and too little time and energy on everything else — thinking, reading, speaking, and meeting the voters. In a 1988 study by the Center, *Congress Speaks — A Survey of the 100th Congress*, nearly half of the members of Congress said they would like to spend less time on fundraising.

---

[1] S. Rep. No. 1539, 86th Congress, 2nd Sess. p. 3 (1960).

Sixty-four percent of Senators and almost 87 percent of Senate personal staff said raising money affected the time they spent on legislative work.[2] Any political broadcasting reforms that would help reduce this fundraising burden would therefore help improve Congress as an institution.

The high cost of air time also detracts from the ability of a campaign to inform and educate the public. As a 1959 Senate report put it, "An informed public is indispensable for the continuance of an alert and knowledgeable democratic society."[3] Yet survey results suggest that today, more than ever, candidates fail to reach and inform large portions of the voting public. A 1987 National Opinion Research Center poll found that only 38 percent of the public could name their representative. A CBS/New York Times poll found that in 1982, when the Democrats controlled the House of Representatives, 64 percent of Americans either mistakenly believed the Republicans controlled the House, or did not know. Given such general unfamiliarity with Congress, it is little wonder that voter turnout in 1986 dropped to its lowest level since World War II — only one of three voting-age Americans cast a ballot for a candidate for the House of Representatives.

No single approach can alone address all these concerns adequately. Any policy in this area must balance the free speech rights of the candidates with those of the radio, TV and cable owners. But, the same government which so vigilantly guards any erosion of an individual's freedom of speech also must affirmatively *foster* the free speech of those who would represent us. Nor can effective change come solely from the imposition of new mandatory requirements on media owners. In keeping with the traditions of our country's electoral system — a system fueled by private, voluntary contributions — much of the new political programming should grow out of voluntary efforts by broadcasters, cable operators, charities and foundations, labor unions and corporations. Yet voluntarism cannot do it all. As has been recognized since the Communications Act was signed into law in 1934, federal regulation has an inescapable role to play in determining use of the electronic media in campaigns.

Taken as a whole, the recommendations made in this study, including those on free media, discounted advertising, and a reduction in the restrictions on voluntary programming by stations, would help reduce campaign costs, and significantly increase candidates' ability to talk about the issues with the voter. They would help create a better informed electorate, which in the end can only mean a better, more responsive Congress.

---

[2] Center for Responsive Politics, *Congress Speaks: A Survey of the 100th Congress*, Washington, D.C., 1988, p.65 and p. 82.

[3] S. Rep. No. 560, 86th Cong. 1st Sess. pp. 9-10 (1959).

Appendix A

Full Text and Overall Results of the Center's Survey: Media Use in Congressional Elections

1. a) During the 1986 campaign were you offered any type of free broadcast time or other media, other than debates, newscasts or news interview programs?

    14.7 yes   *83.1* no   *2.3* not sure[1]

   b) If yes, in what format was the time offered? *[2]

   c) Was your opponent offered equal time?

    63.0 yes   *22.2* no   *14.8* not sure

2. a) During the 1986 campaign, on which type of communication did your campaign spend the most money?

    50.6 commercial TV
    — cable TV
    17.8 radio
    7.5 newspapers
    23.0 direct mail

   b) Please estimate how much money your campaign spent on *direct* advertising costs in the 1986 general election campaign.

$ (thousands)	Commercial TV	Radio	Cable TV
$0-10	46.0	64.1	83.1
$10-50	14.7	22.4	8.7
$50-100	13.5	9.6	5.0
$100-250	10.4	3.2	3.1
$250-500	5.5	0.6	0.0
$500-1 Mil	5.5	0.0	0.0
$1 Mil-2 Mil	2.5	0.0	0.0
$2 Mil +	0.0	0.0	0.0

---

[1] Answers expressed in percentages
2. All answers indicated by the asterisk (*) were open-ended questions which could not be statistically tallied.

c) When you purchased paid broadcast time:

1) Roughly, what percentage of your advertising time was in prime time television or "drive time" radio?

50 television   *70* radio   (Results expressed as a median)

2) Did you prefer to purchase higher priced, nonpreemptible advertising time, or lower cost preemptible time?

Nonpreemptible *54.2*
Preemptible *28.0*
Both *17.8*

Why or why not?   *

3) Did you ever seek time at the "lowest unit rate" available by law to all federal candidates?

63.4 yes   *17.9* no   *18.6* not sure

4) If so, did the broadcast station grant your request for such discounted rates?

73.0 yes   *7.0* no   *17.4* sometimes   *2.6* not sure

Why or why not?   *

5) Did you attempt to buy air time in time periods longer than the standard 30/60 second slots?

12.7 yes   *87.3* no

6) If yes, how many time slots and for what length of time?

# of Slots	# of Responses	Time (in secs)	# of Responses
1	*4*	*90*	*1*
2	*2*	*120*	*4*
3	*1*	*180*	*2*
4	*1*	*600*	*1*

7) If so, did the stations grant your request?

9.9 yes   *0.0* no   *90.1* not applicable

3. a) Overall were you satisfied with your dealings with broadcasters in the following respects?

   1) Availability of air time, in general

      92.5 yes   *4.8* no   *2.7* no opinion

   2) Time of day your commercials appeared

      90.3 yes   *3.4* no   *6.2* no opinion

   3) Prices charged

      79.0 yes   *12.6* no   *8.4* no opinion

   b) What suggestions, if any, do you have for changing the way broadcasters sell time to candidates?
   *

4. a) Did any station offer you free time to debate your opponent during either the 1986 primary or general election period?

      72.7 yes   *25.6* no   *1.7* not sure

   b) Was the offer made during the primary or general election period?

      1.6 Primary   *82.8* General   *15.6* Both

   c) If yes, **in each case**: (results listed here are for *general* elections only)

   1) Was the proposed debate to be on commercial, public, or cable television, commercial or public radio?

Commercial TV	25.2	Commercial Radio	10.2
Public TV	18.0	Public Radio	3.1
Cable TV	7.1	TV/Radio Combination	22.0
TV Combination	14.2		

   2) How much time were you offered?

      60 min (result expressed as median)

   3) Was the time offered in prime time?

      54.8 yes   *30.2* no   *11.1* not sure   *4.0* Both

   4) Was the debate actually held?

      65.6 yes   *25.0* no   *0.8* not sure   *8.6* yes & no

5) Do you feel the debate helped your candidate?

72.4 yes   *17.3* no   *10.2* no opinion

Why or why not? *

5. Did you ever decline to participate in a broadcast debate in 1986?

22.7 yes   *72.7* no   *4.7* not sure

Why or why not? *

6. a) Would you favor providing free or discounted time to candidates on radio, television, or cable in one or more of the following ways?

   1) Require broadcasters to provide free time for the use of candidates.

      45.4 yes   *45.4* no   *9.2* no opinion

   2) Have the federal government pay the cost of broadcast time for use of candidates.

      16.4 yes   *74.3* no   *9.4* no opinion

   3) Require broadcasters to sell both nonpreemptible and preemptible time at a substantially discounted rate to candidates.

      46.2 yes   *38.5* no   *15.4* no opinion

b) If free or discounted time is provided, should such time be offered to third party candidates?

   62.5 yes   *22.0* no   *15.5* no opinion

c) Would you require broadcasters to at least set aside a specific day before the election when all stations would have to simultaneously provide time to various candidates?

   27.6 yes   *58.2* no   *14.1* no opinion

d) Would you require broadcasters to provide at least some of the free time to candidates to be used for debates?

   58.5 yes   *29.2* no   *12.1* no opinion

7. If Congress decides to enact a new law providing free or discounted time to candidates, certain conditions may be attached to the use of free time or discounted time. How would you feel about conditioning free or discounted time on the following:

a) Candidates agreeing not to spend any additional funds to buy additional air time?

20.7 strongly oppose   *30.5* oppose   *10.4* no opinion

26.8 support   *11.6* strongly support

b) Candidates accepting an aggregate spending limit for the entire campaign?

16.5 strongly oppose   *17.7* oppose   *11.0* no opinion

35.4 support   *19.5* strongly support

c) Candidates accepting a ban on contributions from political action committees?

20.2 strongly oppose   *38.0* oppose   *10.4* no opinion

16.6 support   *14.7* strongly support

d) Candidates accepting certain content regulations, such as requiring a candidate to appear personally in at least 75% of the air time used?

12.7 strongly oppose   *22.9* oppose   *19.9* no opinion

24.7 support   *19.9* strongly support

e) Candidates agreeing to use the free time in blocks at least five minutes long?

11.0 strongly oppose   *27.0* oppose   *31.3* no opinion

22.1 support   *8.6* strongly support

8. Some free media proposals seek to overcome the unique logistical problems of providing free time in media markets with a large number of races. How would you feel about the following?

a) Require broadcasters to give the free time to the House and Senate campaign committees of both national political parties (rather than candidates themselves) to allocate among candidates as they decide.

   22.5 yes   *63.3* no   *14.2* no opinion

b) Require the FCC to allocate the free time among the stations, so that no one station has to provide time for all the candidates.

   49.7 yes   *34.7* no   *15.6* no opinion

c) Permit broadcasters to allocate the air time of candidates among themselves, so that no one station has to provide time for all the races.

   50.6 yes   *33.7* no   *15.7* no opinion

d) Provide postage subsidies or newspaper advertising subsidies as an alternative to free air time for candidates.

   29.5 yes   *56.6* no   *13.9* no opinion

9. Some proposals seek to modify some of the current laws in order to encourage broadcasters to act voluntarily to provide more free air time for candidates. How do you feel about the following:

a) Repeal the equal time doctrine which requires broadcasters to offer comparable time at comparable rates to all candidates, if it is offered to one candidate?

   31.8 strongly oppose   *39.4* oppose   *12.4* no opinion

   7.6 support   *8.8* strongly support

b) Exclude minor third party candidates from the equal time rules to allow broadcasters to present major party candidates in any format without incurring an obligation to offer time to minor party candidates as well?

   13.7 strongly oppose   *38.7* oppose   *17.9* no opinion

   23.2 support   *6.5* strongly support

c) Permit broadcasters who organize a debate to air the program even if only one of the candidates chooses to participate, without having to provide the other candidate equal time at a later date?

    8.3 strongly oppose   *18.9* oppose   *11.8* no opinion

    36.1 support   *24.9* strongly support

d) Permit broadcasters and other media companies to grant free time for advertisements to major party candidates without it being considered a corporate contribution under the federal election laws?

    17.3 strongly oppose   *25.6* oppose   *14.3* no opinion

    31.0 support   *11.9* strongly support

10. Do you have any thoughts or suggestions on how the broadcast media could be used to inform the public about candidates and the issues?

*

Appendix B

Excerpts from Communications Act of 1934 and Implementing Regulations

PART I
COMMUNICATIONS ACT OF 1934, AS AMENDED

1.§ 312. Administrative sanctions (47 USC 312)

(a) **Revocation of station license or construction permit**

The Commission may revoke any station license or construction permit...

(7) for willful or repeated failure to allow reasonable access to or to permit purchase of reasonable amounts of time for the use of a broadcasting station by a legally qualified candidate for Federal elective office on behalf of his candidacy...

(b) - (e) ...

(f) **Willful or repeated violations**

For purposes of this section:

(1) The term "willful", when used with reference to the commission or omission of any act, means the conscious and deliberate commission or omission of such act, irrespective of any intent to violate any provision of this chapter or any rule or regulation of the Commission authorized by this chapter or by a treaty ratified by the United States.

(2) The term "repeated", when used with reference to the commission or omission of any act, means the commission or omission of such act more than once or, if such commission or omission is continuous, for more than one day.

2. §315. Candidates for public office (47 USC 315)

(a) **Equal opportunities requirement; censorship prohibition; allowance of station use; news appearances exception; public interest; public issues discussion opportunities**

If any licensee shall permit any person who is a legally qualified candidate for any public office to use a broadcasting station, he shall afford equal opportunities to all other such candidates for that office in the use of such broadcasting station: *Provided*, That such licensee shall have no power of censorship over the material broadcast under the provisions of this section. No obligation is imposed under this subsection upon any licensee to allow the use of its station by any such candidate. Appearance by a legal qualified candidate on any --

(1) bona fide newscast

(2) bona fide news interview

(3) bona fide news documentary (if the appearance of the candidate is incidental to the presentation of the subject or subjects covered by the news documentary), or

(4) on-the-spot coverage of bona fide events (including but not limited to political conventions and activities incidental thereto),

shall not be deemed to be use of a broadcasting station within the meaning of this subsection. Nothing in the foregoing sentence shall be construed as relieving broadcasters, in connection with the presentation of newscasts, news interviews, news documentaries, and on-the-spot coverage of news events, from the obligation imposed upon them under this chapter to operate in the public interest and to afford reasonable opportunity for the discussion of conflicting views on issues of public importance.

(b) **Broadcast media rates**

The charges made for the use of any broadcasting station by any person who is a legally qualified candidate for any public office in connection with his campaign for nomination for election, or election to such office shall not exceed—
(1) during the forty-five days preceding the date of a primary or primary runoff election and during the sixty days preceding the date of a general or special election in which such person is a candidate, the lowest unit charge of the station for the same class and amount of time for the same period; and

(2) at any other time, the charges made for comparable use of such station by other users thereof.

(c) **Definitions**

For purposes of this section -

(1) the term "broadcasting station" includes a community antenna television system; and

(2) the terms "licensee" and "station licensee" when used with respect to a community antenna television system mean the operator of such system.

(d) **Rules and regulations**

The Commission shall prescribe appropriate rules and regulations to carry out the provisions of this section.

PART II
FCC IMPLEMENTING REGULATIONS

1. § 73.1940. Broadcasts by candidates for public office

(a) . . .

(b) **Charges for use of stations.** The charges, if any, made for the use of any broadcasting station by any person who is a legally qualified candidate for any public office in connection with his campaign for nomination for election, or election, to such office shall not exceed

(1) During the 45 days preceding the date of a primary or primary runoff election and during the 60 days preceding the date of a general or special election in which such person is a candidate, the lowest unit charge of the station for the same class and amount of time for the same period, and

(2) At any other time the charges made for comparable use of such station by other users thereof. The rates, if any, charged all such candidates for the same office shall be uniform and shall not be rebated by any means direct or indirect. A candidate shall be charged no more than the rate the station would charge if the candidate were a commercial advertiser whose advertising was directed to promoting its business within the same area as that encompassed by the particular office for which such person is a candidate. All discount privileges otherwise offered by a station to commercial advertisers shall be available upon equal terms to all candidates for public office.

(3) This paragraph shall not apply to any station which is not licensed for commercial operation.

(c) Discrimination between candidates. In making time available to candidates for public office, no licensee shall make any discrimination between candidates in practices, regulations, facilities, or services for or in connection with the service rendered pursuant to this part, or make or give any preference to any candidate for public office or subject any such candidate to any prejudice or disadvantage; nor shall any licensee make any contract or other agreement which shall have the effect of permitting any legally qualified candidate for any public office to broadcast to the exclusion of other legally qualified candidates for the same public office.

(d) Records, inspection. Every licensee shall keep and permit public inspection of a complete record (political file) of all requests for broadcast time made by or on behalf of candidates for public office, together with an appropriate notation showing the disposition made by the licensee of such requests, and the charges made, if any, if the request is granted. When free time is provided for use by or on behalf of such candidates, a record of the free time provided shall be placed in the political file. All records required by this paragraph shall be placed in the political file as soon as possible and shall be retained for a period of two years. See §§ 73.3526 and 73.3527.

(e) Time of request. A request for equal opportunities must be submitted to the licensee within 1 week of the day on which the first prior use, giving rise to the right of equal opportunities, occurred: *Provided, however,* that where the person was not a candidate at the time of such first prior use, he shall submit his request within 1 week of the first subsequent use after he has become a legally qualified candidate for the office in question.

(f) Burden of proof. A candidate requesting equal opportunities of the licensee, or complaining of noncompliance to the Commission shall have the burden of proving that he and his opponent are legally qualified candidates for the same public office.

(g) General requirements.

(1) Except as otherwise indicated in paragraph (g)(2) of this section, no station licensee is required to permit the use of its facilities by any legally qualified candidate for public office, but if any licensee shall permit any such candidate to use its facilities, it shall afford equal opportunities to all other candidates for that office to use such facilities. Such licensee shall have no power of censorship over the material broadcast by any such candidate. Appearance by a legally qualified candidate on any: (i) Bona fide newscast; (ii) bona fide news interview; (iii) bona fide news documentary (if the appearance of the candidate is incidental to the presentation of the subject or subjects covered by the news documentary); or (iv) on-the-spot coverage of bona fide news

events (including, but not limited to political conventions and activities incidental thereto) shall not be deemed to be use of a broadcasting station. (Section 315(a) of the Communications Act.)

(2) Section 312(a)(7) of the Communications Act provides that the Commission may revoke any station license or construction permit for willful or repeated failure to allow reasonable access to, or to permit purchase of, reasonable amounts of time for the use of a broadcasting station by a legally qualified candidate for Federal elective office on behalf of his candidacy.

(h) Political broadcasting primer. A detailed study of these rules regarding broadcasts by candidates for Federal and non-Federal public office is available in the FCC public notice of July 20, 1978, "The Law of Political Broadcasting and Cablecasting." Copies may be obtained from the FCC upon request.

2. § 76.5 Cable television service definitions

(a) - (q) ...

(r) Origination cablecasting. Programming (exclusive of broadcast signals) carried on a cable television system over one or more channels and subject to the exclusive control of the cable operator.

3. § 76.205 Origination cablecasts by candidates for public office

(a) General requirements. If a cable television system operator shall permit any legally qualified candidate for public office to use the system's cablecasting channel(s) and facilities therefor, the system operator shall afford equal opportunities to all other such candidates for that office: *Provided, however,* That such cable television system operator shall have no power of censorship over the material cablecast by any such candidate: *And provided, further,* That an appearance by a legally qualified candidate on any:

(1) Bona fide newscast,

(2) Bona fide news interview,

(3) Bona fide news documentary (if the appearance of the candidate is incidental to the presentation of the subject or subjects covered by the news documentary), or

(4) On-the-spot coverage of bona fide news events (including but not limited to political conventions and activities incidental thereto), shall not be deemed to be use of the facilities of the system within the meaning of this paragraph.

Note: The fairness doctrine is applicable to these exempt categories. See § 76.209.

(b) Charges for use of cable systems. The charges, if any, made for the use of any cable television system by any person who is a legally qualified candidate for any public office in connection with his campaign for nomination for election, or election, to such office shall not exceed:

> (1) During the 45 days preceding the date of a primary or primary runoff election and during the 60 days preceding the date of a general or special election in which such is a candidate, the lowest unit charge of the cable television system for the same class and amount of time for the same period, and

> (2) At any other time the charges made for comparable use of such system by other users thereof. The rates, if any, charged all such candidates for the same office shall be uniform and shall not be rebated by any means direct or indirect. A candidate shall be charged no more than the rate the cable television system would charge if the candidate were a commercial advertiser whose advertising was directed to promoting its business within the same area as that encompassed by the particular office for which such person is a candidate. All discount privileges otherwise offered by a cable television system to commercial advertisers shall be available upon equal terms to candidates for public office.

(c) Discrimination between candidates. In making time available to candidates for public office, no cable television system operator shall make any discrimination between candidates in practices, regulations, facilities, or services for or in connection with the service rendered pursuant to this part, or make or give any preference to any candidate for public office or subject any such candidate to any prejudice or disadvantage; nor shall any cable television system operator make any contract or other agreement which shall have the effect of permitting any legally qualified candidate for any public office to cablecast to the exclusion of other legally qualified candidates for the same public office.

(d) Records, inspection. Every cable television system operator shall keep and permit public inspection of a complete record (political file) of all requests for cablecast time made by or on behalf of candidates for public office, together with an appropriate notation showing the disposition made by the cable television system operator of such requests, and the charges made, if any, if request is granted. When free time is provided for use by or on behalf of such candidates, a record of the free time provided shall be placed in the political file. All records required by this paragraph shall be placed in the political file as soon as possible and shall be retained for a period of two years.

(e) Time of request. A request for equal opportunities for use of the origination channel(s) must be submitted to the cable television system operator within one (1) week of the day on which the first prior use, giving rise to the right of equal opportunities, occurred: *Provided, however,* That where a person was not a candidate at the time of such first prior use, he shall submit his request within one (1) week of the first subsequent use after he has become a legally qualified candidate for the office in question.

(f) Burden of proof. A candidate requesting such equal opportunities of the cable television system operator, or complaining of noncompliance to the Commission, shall have the burden of proving that he and his opponent are legally qualified candidates for the same public office.